The Polyphony of Life

The Polyphony of Life

BONHOEFFER'S THEOLOGY OF MUSIC

Andreas Pangritz

Edited by
John W. de Gruchy and John Morris

Translated by
Robert Steiner

CASCADE *Books* · Eugene, Oregon

THE POLYPHONY OF LIFE
Bonhoeffer's Theology of Music

Cascade Books
An Imprint of Wipf and Stock Publishers
199 W. 8th Ave., Suite 3
Eugene, OR 97401

www.wipfandstock.com

PAPERBACK ISBN: 978-1-5326-6152-5
HARDCOVER ISBN: 978-1-5326-6153-2
EBOOK ISBN: 978-1-5326-6154-9

Cataloguing-in-Publication data:

Names: Pangritz, Andreas, author. | De Gruchy, John W., editor. | Morris, John, editor. | Steiner, Robert, translator.

Title: The polyphony of life : Bonhoeffer's theology of music / Andreas Pangritz ; .

Description: Eugene, OR: Cascade Books, 2019. | Includes bibliographical references and index.

Identifiers: ISBN 978-1-5326-6152-5 (paperback). | ISBN 978-1-5326-6153-2 (hardcover). | ISBN 978-1-5326-6154-9 (ebook).

Subjects: LCSH: Bonhoeffer, Dietrich—1906-1945. | Music—Religious aspects—Christianity. | Music—Philosophy and aesthetics. | Theology, Doctrinal—History.

Classification: BX4827.B57 P36131 2019 (print). | BS4827 (ebook).

Manufactured in the U.S.A.   OCTOBER 7, 2019

This volume is a translation from the German second edition of *Polyphonie des Lebens: Zu Dietrich Bonhoeffers "Theologie der Musik,"* Dahlemer Heft 13 (Berlin: Orient & Okzident, 2000).

Contents

Preface to the English Translation

𝄞

THIS STUDY HAD ORIGINALLY been conceived in 1984 on the occasion of Eberhard Bethge's seventy-fifth birthday. It was received by Bethge with friendly comments; however, no publisher was interested in printing it. Perhaps the topic of Bonhoeffer's theological reflections on music seemed too exotic at that time.

Ten years later, on the occasion of Bethge's eighty-fifth birthday, I decided to publish the manuscript in a slightly revised version at my own expense. This first edition was designed to celebrate the jubilee of a person representing the "polyphony of life," who himself had an important share in developing Bonhoeffer's theology of music.

A few months after Bethge's death a revised second edition appeared in 2000 on the occasion of the Eighth International Bonhoeffer Congress in Berlin. A special problem was posed by Bonhoeffer's quotations of musical notations. Their reproduction in Dietrich Bonhoeffer Works, volume 8 (*Letters and Papers from Prison*) is not in accordance with Bonhoeffer's manuscript and suggests nonsense. They had to be revised.

Parts of the book, mostly taken from the chapters on Heinrich Schütz and on *The Art of Fugue*, have been published earlier in my own paraphrasing translation as "Point and Counterpoint—Resistance and Submission: Dietrich Bonhoeffer on Theology and

Music in Times of War and Social Crisis," in *Theology in Dialogue: The Impact of the Art, Humanities, and Science on Contemporary Religious Thought* (Essays in Honor of John W. de Gruchy), edited by Lyn Holness and Ralf K. Wüstenberg.

It is an honor to me that a few years ago I was asked for permission to prepare an English translation. My agreement included the permission to rearrange some complicated passages and footnotes in order to make the book more readable. I am very happy about the outcome. In some respects the English translation is better than the German original. Many thanks to the translators! And thanks to Cascade Books for their immediate readiness to publish this translation! Particular thanks go especially to those who have been involved in bringing the project to completion: James Stock, Daniel Lanning, Matthew Wimer, Jeremy Funk, George Callihan, and K. C. Hanson.

The English version appears on occasion of the Thirteenth International Bonhoeffer Congress in Stellenbosch, South Africa, in January 2020.

ANDREAS PANGRITZ
Bonn, May 2019

Editors' Introduction

John W. de Gruchy

Dietrich Bonhoeffer did not write a book or give lectures on music like his mentor Karl Barth, whose little collection of essays on Mozart are always a delight to read.[1] But music was a dominant feature of Bonhoeffer's life. Not only was he an accomplished musician himself, he was also very knowledgeable about music. Above all he enjoyed music, and especially making music with others. All of this is well known to those who have an interest in Bonhoeffer's legacy. What is less known, and seldom acknowledged, is the role music played in shaping the development of his theology. It is precisely this lacuna in Bonhoeffer studies that Andreas Pangritz's little book *Polyphonie des Lebens* filled when it first appeared in 1994.[2] I read it soon after, and it became a seminal text for me in thinking about what Bonhoeffer meant when, in prison, he wrote about the need to recover "aesthetic existence" in the life of the church. And this, in turn, helped me to see the integral connection between "aesthetic existence" and the Christian life and

1. Barth, *Wolfgang Amadeus Mozart.*
2. Pangritz, *Polyphonie.*

discipleship, a novel yet refreshing insight which, when introduced to students, found an immediate and positive response. From then on, the seed was sown to making *Polyphonie* accessible to English readers who could either not read German, or might find Pangritz's text very dense, terse, and scholarly beyond their ability to grasp. And that would, I mused, be a great pity, for *Polyphonie* is a treasure to be savored. That it is an important text to read and savor was reinforced when, in 2000, a new and revised German edition was published and dedicated to Bonhoeffer's close friend Eberhard Bethge, who died that same year.

For a variety of reasons, I delayed almost twenty years before pursuing the idea of translating *Polyphonie* into English. But the seed planted back in 1994 suddenly germinated when, in 2017, I became friends with John Morris, a trained historian, bibliophile, and accomplished musician, and introduced him to Bonhoeffer's life and thought. John was entranced by Bonhoeffer's story, and excited to discover that he shared Bonhoeffer's passion for music. At the same time, he introduced me to the history and theory of music in a way that helped me to understand music as never before. *Polyphonie des Lebens* was soon taken down off my bookshelf to be read again, and it was then that the seed planted in 1994 began to sprout as John and I decide to embark together on the task of producing a readable English version. I immediately wrote to Andreas, with whom I have had a long friendship, to suggest doing so, and he was immediately enthusiastic. In no time we had secured the interest of Wipf and Stock Publishers, which had previously published books written by us both.

To be honest, my German was not up to doing the translation, so I proposed that this task be undertaken by a mutual friend, Robert Steiner, minister of the Rondebosch United Church in Cape Town. Robert, who wrote his PhD dissertation on Bonhoeffer at the University of Cape Town, was also immediately enthusiastic. But even he, a German speaker, soon discovered that translating the text was no simple matter, for its structure, vocabulary, and content were more demanding than any of us had previously imagined. In fact, its size is deceptive, for every word and sentence demands the careful consideration and reflection we would normally give to a much more extensive scientific treatise. Nonetheless, the task of translating, editing, and making it as accessible as possible for English readers, has proved to be a demanding adventure, but one well worth the effort.

In making the book more readable, and with Pangritz's warm approval, we have not produced a literal translation of the text, but it is, we believe, faithful to the original. One of the major changes is that we have lifted several, though not all, of the lengthy quotations from the extensive footnotes and placed then in the text itself. Many of these footnotes, both those we have placed in the text and those that remain where they originally were, are not available in English translation, so we have translated these as well while leaving the references to the German originals. But all the Bonhoeffer quotations are taken from the volumes of the Dietrich Bonhoeffer Works in English (DBWE), which we duly acknowledge with gratitude.

As previously mentioned, Andreas dedicated *Polyphonie* to Eberhard Bethge, Bonhoeffer's trusted friend, biographer, and interpreter. As Bethge was mentor to both Pangritz and to myself, as well as being our wonderful elder friend, there is every reason to dedicate this English edition to him as well. Bethge did a great deal to bridge the gap between German and English Bonhoeffer scholarship, and it is our hope that this book will be a further symbol of this important and mutually stimulating relationship.

Bonhoeffer's Little Invention

John Morris

THIS SLIM VOLUME, ORIGINALLY published twenty-five years ago in German, in many ways constitutes a remarkable précis of a vast body of work devoted to the theology of Dietrich Bonhoeffer. Distilling many of the ideas that preoccupied him in prison during his final year, it can be regarded as a summary of an idea at the very core of his thinking. The fragmentary nature of life, he discovered, finds a metaphor in music. He shared his "little discovery" (*Fundlein*) with Eberhard Bethge in a series of letters written in the spring of 1944, at which time he had been held at Tegel prison for over twelve months.

The way this evidently accomplished musician melded his theology with his understanding of music provides, for me, a very welcome and special understanding of his life and thought. It is remarkable that music should have preoccupied him at all, given the restrictions placed upon him. He was sufficiently familiar with many works to be able to hear them silently, in his own head, so to speak. But the privations he suffered thus also gave him an added insight into the experience of Beethoven, whose deafness necessitated a similar inward journey.

The privilege of working on this translation has been all the more rewarding because just as *Polyphony of Life* introduces Andreas Pangritz to a wider English-speaking readership, so this translation provides me with a unique introduction to Bonhoeffer. My personal interest in Dietrich Bonhoeffer is the result of my recently established friendship with John de Gruchy, with whom I have spent many months editing this text (sympathetically translated by Robert Steiner). Whereas I come at the subject from a music historiography point of view, John brings his lifetime of work on Bonhoeffer's theology, and I have also been struck by the conclusions that Bonhoeffer draws with regard to a "religionless Christianity," to which during the course of my research I have found in Ralph Vaughan Williams a musical parallel to Bonhoeffer (and an Anglo-Saxon one).

My own sphere of interest is in British music and politics in the period between the wars and it was a delight to discover that Bonhoeffer was in London for the whole of 1934. During his pastorship in Sydenham he acquired a British recording of Bach's B Minor Mass (which he later confessed was one of his favorite works). It is tempting to speculate whether he was able to attend a performance of the work that took place in Whitechapel in September of that year, and whether he attended any concerts at the Queen's Hall that year, including Proms performances, that by then were already in their fortieth year. Had he done so he may, for example, have heard the first performance of Ralph Vaughan Williams's *Fantasia on Greensleeves* that summer. Given *his* interest in J. S. Bach it would be just as intriguing to know if Vaughan Williams was at that same performance of the B Minor Mass.

What musical experiences Bonhoeffer might have enjoyed in London during his ministry at Sydenham can only be conjectured, as no record exists, whether in the form of either a diary entry or a letter home, of any musical excursions he may have made. That Bonhoeffer would have had access to a wireless during his extended stay in London during 1934 is without question however, and the BBC was not only broadcasting a considerable output of serious music, but was also pioneering new music. One can only imagine the interest Bonhoeffer may have taken in a pioneering broadcast of Alban Berg's *Wozzeck*, for example. That Vaughan Williams was active at the very time Bonhoeffer was in London for me is an appealing idea.

A self-confessed agnostic, Vaughan Williams was nevertheless drawn to biblical texts. (*Flos Campi*, completed in 1925, is a suite in six movements for solo viola, wordless choir, and small orchestra, each of which is headed by a verse from the Song of Solomon, that perplexing book of the Old Testament that also interested Bonhoeffer so much during his final year.) Vaughan Williams found lifelong inspiration in *The Pilgrim's Progress* and wrote some of the finest hymn tunes in *The English Hymnal*, which he edited, and which was published in 1906 (coincidentally, the year of Bonhoeffer's birth).

Vaughan Williams spent a lifetime engaged with the work of John Bunyan (1628–1688) and found inspiration there for many works. His use of the church modes (particularly during the war) was quite deliberate, to evoke a bygone era that drew on a deep English spirituality. In his opera (or, as he preferred to call it a "Morality"), *The Pilgrim's Progress,* he purposely did not call the Pilgrim Christian, the name given to the hero by Bunyan. Rather, as he revealed in a letter, he wanted the opera, which occupied him for much of his life "to be universal and apply to any body *[sic]* who aims at the spiritual life whether he is Xtian, Jew, Buddhist, Shintoist or 5th *[sic]* day Adventist."[1] This is, surely, akin to Bonhoeffer's religionless Christianity.

The serenity at the heart of Vaughan Williams's Fifth Symphony, which contains much of the same thematic material as the later Morality and first performed in 1943, was inspired by the crucifixion. Although the composer later deleted them, he inscribed on the original manuscript of the slow movement words from Bunyan: "Upon this place stood a cross, and a little below a sepulchre. Then he said: 'He hath given me rest by his sorrow,

1. Cobbe, ed., *Letters of Ralph Vaughan Williams*, 485.

and life by his death.'" In this music he distilled all that he knew of English modality—formal Elizabethan music as well as folk—into one sublime movement. What is at its heart? In it "the parallel, organum-like, dark chords heard in the lower wind and strings reflect perhaps the sepulchre in the deleted Bunyan superscription."[2] Does it matter that he scratched out that superscription? Wilfrid Mellers has written that the composer no doubt felt that "the music stood on its own and would be unnecessarily circumscribed by a seventeenth-century text."[3] Regarded by Michael Kennedy as "one of the high peaks of English romantic symphonic art," at the heart of the *Romanza* lies Pilgrim's "Save me Lord! My burden is greater than I can bear."[4] I would venture that Vaughan Williams thus epitomises Bonhoeffer's "unconscious Christianity." And this from a man whose self-declared agnosticism seems entirely at home with Bonhoeffer's come-of-age Christianity, and he does it, happily for us, though music.

Bonhoeffer is thus introduced to me from a musical point of view, perhaps through a relatively arcane introduction to a life that has been documented extensively and studied widely, and through a text that explores the very last ideas he had about what it means to be Christian in a world that has "come of age." That my own introduction to Bonhoeffer, which this translation has enabled has come through the lens of music, is more personally significant because I have discovered how a gifted theologian meets Germany's greatest contemporary novelist (Thomas Mann), and both agree with a composer who has been the subject of my own research of the same period.

Vaughan Williams, who had done much to revive Bach's music (particularly the *Saint Matthew Passion*, much as Felix Mendelssohn had done a hundred years before), clearly also held Beethoven in the highest regard and, indeed, in the early months of the war went on the radio to explain to an antagonized audience

---

2. Hedley, "Vaughan Williams," 7.

3. Mellers, *Vaughan Williams and the Vision of Albion*, 181.

4. Kennedy, *Works of Ralph Vaughan Williams*, 282.

why the music of Beethoven belonged to the *free* peoples of the world and therefore should not be banned from being broadcast by the BBC, despite some calls to do so. After Vaughan Williams had ably defended German music, and Beethoven especially, that composer's work came to exemplify freedom itself and became a symbol of victory. It is intriguing to know that while Bonhoeffer was languishing in jail thinking about Beethoven's last works, Vaughan Williams and others in Britain were claiming Beethoven and wresting his memory from the Nazis, who preferred to think of Beethoven as a the ultimate expression of German natural superiority.

It is notable that during his incarceration, Bonhoeffer should have returned to where he began—a young, highly gifted musician who chose the path of theology—that he turned to Bach (especially the B Minor Mass, and the *Saint Matthew Passion*) and to Beethoven (particularly the final piano sonata, opus 111). But it was *The Art of Fugue*, however, that provided him with the metaphor of the interweaving, fragmentary nature of life itself. In his contribution to the volume of essays in honor of John de Gruchy on his retirement, Andreas Pangritz has written that the notion of the polyphony of life, "conceived by Bonhoeffer as a musical description of a Christian life, does not mean harmony without conflict or dissonance. Rather it includes the perception of light and shadow, of love and suffering, of longing and passion amidst social [and personal, given Bonhoeffer's comments on the sensual] crisis and catastrophe. In other words it contains both aspects of hope: hopeful resistance against fate and submission to God's will, full of hope as well."[5]

Some translations, not least John de Gruchy's own *Christianity, Art and Transformation* refer to Bonhoeffer's "little invention,"[6] which suggests another musical allusion—to that of Bach's Two- and Three-Part Inventions BWV 772–801, those beginner's introductions to counterpoint known by every budding pianist.

5. Pangritz, *Polyphonie*, 42.

6. De Gruchy, *Christianity, Art and Transformation*, 160.

This *Fundlein* or "little discovery" (translated as "hobbyhorse" in DBWE) for me is no "little" discovery at all. Bonhoeffer found in music an answer to a question that had been bothering him. Where did transcendence truly lie? This, of course, is also the subject of Thomas Mann's *Doctor Faustus*, which has been the subject of a parallel research trajectory (and explored by John de Gruchy in the forthcoming *Festschrift* in honour of Andreas Pangritz to be published by Kohlhammer in 2020). And whereas the antihero composer Adrian Leverkühn reaches into the ultimate and pays with his sanity, Bonhoeffer discovered that transcendence was, paradoxically, to be found in the here and now, in the world, in the penultimate.

At the end of his life, Bonhoeffer is in prison contemplating Beethoven. Despite knowing his fate, Bonhoeffer understood Beethoven's final piano sonata, and this understanding contributes to his serenity at a moment in history that has great significance. For just as the music reaches its goal, it draws back. There is nothing more to be said.

Elsewhere, Andreas Pangritz has argued that an understanding of Bonhoeffer is impossible without an understanding of how music influenced him. Writes Keith Clements, "He began his musical journey with Beethoven as a teenager, but then ends with him, his incarceration bringing him back to the great master."[7] Clements reminds us of the sermon given on the occasion of the baptism of his nephew Dietrich Bethge:

> Music, as your parents understand and practice it, will bring you back from confusion to your clearest and purest self and perceptions, and from cares and sorrows to the underlying note of joy.[8]

So with this first English translation of Andreas Pangritz's important work, I hope that its publication is no mere "little discovery" for readers, but rather a valuable insight into the musical ideas that occupied Dietrich Bonhoeffer towards the end of his

---

7. Clements, *Bonhoeffer and Britain*, 145.
8. Bonhoeffer, *Letters and Papers from Prison*, 385.

life, and how the example found in polyphony provides for us a concrete basis for understanding the progress of the soul towards transcendence, and how that progress is expressed in music.

Abbreviations

DBWE   Dietrich Bonhoeffer Works in English

ESV   English Standard Version of the Bible

JB   Jerusalem Bible

1

Bonhoeffer's Musical Biography

THERE ARE NUMEROUS SPECULATIVE statements about music in Dietrich Bonhoeffer's *Letters and Papers* from Tegel prison, occasionally supported by musical notations. Most occur prior to Bonhoeffer's discussion of what Eberhard Bethge called his "new theology,"[1] which developed in response to his question, "what is Christianity, or who is Christ actually for us today?"[2] But the references are revealing, for they prelude and provide a commentary on Bonhoeffer's final theological thought which, Bethge noted, was frequently regarded as shocking by those who read it after the Second World War. That Bonhoeffer's last specifically theological reflections were preceded by those on musical terms is, however, no coincidence.

Bonhoeffer was already musically educated in the classical-romantic tradition before his interest in theology developed.[3] In

1. Bethge, *Dietrich Bonhoeffer.* 853–92.

2. Letter of April 30th, 1944. Bonhoeffer, *Letters and Papers from Prison*, 362.

3. See Bethge, *Dietrich Bonhoeffer*, 24–25.

this respect he was typical of his social class, for "making music" at home was an integral part of bourgeois culture. Bonhoeffer was "playing Mozart sonatas at the age of ten," writes Bethge, and "on Saturday evenings he skilfully accompanied his mother and his sister Ursula, who had a good voice, in songs by Schubert, Schumann, Brahms and Hugo Wolf." At an early age, Bethge goes on to say, Bonhoeffer was accustomed "to performing without shyness or embarrassment."[4]

This nineteenth-century musical legacy or "romantic heritage"[5] was imparted to Bonhoeffer by his mother, whose own mother (née Kalckreuth) had enjoyed singing and had taken piano lessons with Clara Schumann and Franz Liszt.[6] In this way a "treasure chest of songs" was handed down to the Bonhoeffer siblings, something Dietrich later recalled in his prison letters. According to Bethge, the young Bonhoeffer had played a "small selection" of the songs of Hugo Wolf with his sister, and later, before his imprisonment, Bethge and Bonhoeffer bought a large quantity of these songs and tried them.[7] It seems that among the siblings it was especially Dietrich to whom the "Kalckreuthian family musicality" was passed on. In addition to the piano, Bonhoeffer appears to have tried the lute and even attempted his own compositions, and he "made such musical and technical progress at the piano that, for a time, both he and his parents thought that he might become a professional musician."[8]

Bonhoeffer's turn to theology never displaced music. Throughout his life he kept his skill as a pianist, especially his ability as an accompanist. He applied both skills during his parish

---

4. Bethge, *Dietrich Bonhoeffer*, 25.

5. Bethge, *Dietrich Bonhoeffer*, 429.

6. Bethge, *Dietrich Bonhoeffer*, 3.

7. Letter to Pangritz from Bethge from 12.9.1984; See Bethge, *Dietrich Bonhoeffer in Selbstzeugnissen*, 16. Cf. Bonhoeffer's repeated references to the songs of Hugo Wolf in Bonhoeffer, *Letters and Papers from Prison*, 68, 70, 251, 319, 327.

8. Bethge, *Dietrich Bonhoeffer*, 25.

work in Barcelona (1928),[9] and in London (1933–1935),[10] as well as when playing chamber music at home, often with his brother-in-law Rüdiger Schleicher on the violin and his brother Klaus on the cello.[11] But a shift in his musical outlook becomes evident after Bonhoeffer increasingly came under the influence of Karl Barth's "Dialectical Theology."[12] The influence of Barth's criticism of religion in his commentary on the *Epistle to the Romans* (second edition 1922),[13] for example, can be seen in Bonhoeffer's critical comment about Beethoven's "quartets and symphonies" in a sermon preached in Barcelona in March 1928 on Rom 11:6:

> There is in the soul of human beings, as truly as they are human beings, something that makes them restless, something that points them toward the infinite, eternal . . . this notion of something eternal, something infinite, makes the soul anxious in its own transitoriness . . . It wants to acquire power over the eternal so that it can rid itself of anxiety and restlessness . . . From this restlessness of the soul the colossal works of philosophy and art emerged.[14]

This "restlessness of soul" is "religion," says Bonhoeffer, but "the sum total of Christianity is not religion, but rather revelation."[15]

Together with his theologically motivated preference for Bach, even though Barth loved Mozart more,[16] Bonhoeffer developed a reservation for the classical-romantic tradition, at least as far as its liturgical use was concerned.[17] In a section on

9. Bethge, *Dietrich Bonhoeffer*, 107.

10. Bethge, *Dietrich Bonhoeffer*, 328.

11. See Bethge, *Dietrich Bonhoeffer in Selbstzeugnissen*, 16. Regarding Bonhoeffer's piano playing see also Johannes Goebel, "When he sat down at the piano," in Zimmerman and Smith, eds., *I Knew Bonhoeffer*, 124.

12. See Pangritz, *Karl Barth*, 15–18.

13. Barth, *Epistle to the Romans*, 547

14. Bonhoeffer, *Barcelona, Berlin, America*, 481–82.

15. Bonhoeffer, *Barcelona, Berlin, America*, 483.

16. See Barth, *Wolfgang Amadeus Mozart*.

17. In view of Barth's preference for Mozart, Bonhoeffer's tendency to play

"The Church and the Proletariat" in his dissertation, *Sanctorum Communio* (1927), which was omitted from the published version (1930),[18] Bonhoeffer raises theological and sociological concerns about the liturgical use of Mendelssohn's music. Playing it was still customary in the 1930s in Berlin's Grunewald congregation where Bonhoeffer grew up. But in his dissertation Bonhoeffer writes that "the coming church will not be 'bourgeois.'" He continues:

> How it will look is today still unclear. It is certain, though, that it is not Thorwaldsen or Mendelssohn who are able to proclaim the importance of the church-community, but rather Dürer, Rembrandt, and Bach.[19]

It has been questioned whether this comment reflects rather an anti-Semitic prejudice against the use of Mendelssohn's "sugary" church music, a perennial prejudice in spite of the fact that it was Mendelssohn himself who had made Bach popular.[20] Undoubtedly Bonhoeffer is, at this point, in dubious company: After all, the removal of Leipzig's Mendelssohn monument at the end of 1936 in the absence of the mayor, Carl Goerdeler, which led to his resignation, was clearly anti-Semitic. However, to Bonhoeffer's credit his early criticism of Mendelssohn, which is not overtly anti-Semitic, was not repeated later, as far as we know.

Beethoven also suffers a similar fate at Bonhoeffer's hands during the church struggle against Nazism. His liturgical use is summarily dismissed by him in a sermon on Cantata Sunday in 1934:

> Bach wrote at the top of all his manuscripts *soli deo Gloria*, or *Jesu juva*,[21] and it is as though Bach's music was nothing other than the untiring praise of God. Beethoven's music, on the other hand, seems to be

---

off Bach theologically against the classical-romantic tradition, must be considered a (significant) misunderstanding of Barth's christological concentration.

18. Bonhoeffer, *Sanctorum Communio*: 271ff.

19. Bonhoeffer, *Sanctorum Communio*, 273

20. Joachim von Soosten, editor of the new German edition of *Sanctorum Communio*, in a letter dated April 1, 1986, to the author.

21. "To God alone be the glory" or "with Jesus' help."—Ed.

nothing but the eternal expression of human suffering and passion. That is why we listen to Bach in church, and not to Beethoven.[22]

Music also played an important role for Bonhoeffer during his time in Finkenwalde. In his report written in 1936 for his students and friends he says: "Now as before, we spend a great deal of time and derive great joy from our music making . . . in general, I can hardly imagine our life together here without our daily music making. We have driven out many an evil spirit in this way."[23]

It is then, finally, that a whole "new world" opened up for Bonhoeffer, when Bethge introduced him to the vocal compositions of the pre-Bach masters, especially those of Heinrich Schütz. Bonhoeffer, writes Bethge, "loved to sing one of the two voices in Schütz's duets *Eins bitte ich vom Herren* [One thing I ask of the Lord] or *Meister, wir haben die ganze Nacht gearbeitet* [Master, we toiled all night]."[24] "At times they spent a few hours a day with this music, especially during the unsettling period of the Resistance and the War, the whole family even practised Schütz cantatas in Schleicher's home."[25] But this new experience by no means diminished Bonhoeffer's passion for Romantic music. As Bethge goes on to say, "his romantic heritage was strongly evident in his playing of Chopin, Brahms, and excerpts from the delightfully stylish *Rosenkavalier*."[26] Together with Bethge, whom he accompanied on the piano, Bonhoeffer at that time played not only Schütz, but also the songs of Hugo Wolf.[27]

Besides the chorales of the hymnbook it is, above all, the world of "polyphony" in Schütz and Bach that unleashes the largest part of Bonhoeffer's musical reflections in his prison letters. In fact, during his imprisonment, a theological rehabilitation of the classical-romantic tradition takes place. Bonhoeffer no longer

22. Bonhoeffer, *London*, 356.

23. Bonhoeffer, *Theological Education at Finkenwalde* 278–79.

24. Bethge, *Dietrich Bonhoeffer*, 429.

25. Bethge, *Bonhoeffer in Selbstzeugnissen,* 16 (author's translation).

26. Bethge, *Dietrich Bonhoeffer*, 429.

27. Bethge, *Bonhoeffer in Selbstzeugnissen,* 16.

looks at it primarily from a liturgical perspective. He refers to Mozart and Hugo Wolf along with Luther and Barth as sharing what he calls *hilaritas* [serenity].[28] And, apart from the music of the late Bach (*The Art of Fugue*), the later music of Beethoven also becomes "existentially appreciated."[29]

28. Bonhoeffer, *Letters and Papers from Prison*, 319.
29. Bonhoeffer, *Letters and Papers from Prison*, 306, 332.

2

Christological Concentration

IN A LETTER TO Ruth Roberta Stahlberg of 23rd March 1940, Bonhoeffer gives an exemplary summary of and a theological justification for his reservations about the musical tradition of his family and class.[1] Reflecting on Bach's *Saint Matthew Passion*, he writes about the "beauty of music" and concludes that only a "beauty that is denied" is true, and that this is the "only possible beauty" for the church. By prefacing his works with *Jesu juva* or *Soli Deo Gloria*, Bach sacrificed at one stroke "all the music's own beauty in and for itself." What is beautiful about the *Saint Matthew Passion* is especially this renunciation of beauty "for the sake of Christ"; here alone "the music . . . comes to itself through Jesus Christ" without desiring "to be anything for itself but everything for Jesus Christ."[2]

The opposition of such music to the abstract and dishonest ideal of beauty in the classical-romantic tradition, or rather, its bourgeois and intellectual reception, is unmistakable. Bonhoeffer

1. Bonhoeffer, *Conspiracy and Imprisonment*, 36–41.
2. Bonhoeffer, *Conspiracy and Imprisonment*, 38.

was disappointed with the church struggle, and this disappointment found its theological expression in the field of music in his letter to Stahlberg. He continues, asking *inter alia*: "is it not those intellectuals who understand more about taste and such matters who have collapsed into such shocking inner turmoil that they are capable in only very rare cases of the simplest deeds of sacrificial love and prayerful action?"[3] However, towards the "ordinary, unimpressive people" Bonhoeffer shows himself surprisingly generous, when he writes:

> Is it not more essential to live and act and die a Christian, singing one's sentimental favorite hymns, than with artfully chosen hymns of the sixteenth century to shy away from the necessary decisions of contemporary Christian existence?[4]

The radical intensification of Bonhoeffer's own position during the church struggle, as reflected in his book *Discipleship* (1937),[5] is expressed in musical terms in the way he comes to suspect even Bach of superficial beauty. He writes: "Whenever in the *St. Matthew Passion* the music begins to desire to be something in itself— I see this in a few of the arias . . . this is the point where it loses its authentic beauty."[6] For Bonhoeffer, Heinrich Schütz is the only one, in whose work no such false beauty can be found. And this, he says, is true for what was then the "latest evangelical church music"[7]—Bonhoeffer names the work of Hugo Distler and Ernst Pepping.[8] Their vast advantage as compared to "other contempo-

3. Bonhoeffer, *Conspiracy and Imprisonment*, 39.

4. Bonhoeffer, *Conspiracy and Imprisonment*, 39.

5. Bonhoeffer, *Discipleship*.

6. Bonhoeffer, *Conspiracy and Imprisonment*, 38.

7. "Evangelical church" refers here to the established Protestant Church in Germany.

8. Hugo Distler (1908–1942) was a church musician and composer; because of the threat of conscription into the German army he committed suicide in 1942 (cf. Bonhoeffer's letter to Distler's widow in Bonhoeffer, *Conspiracy and Imprisonment*. 371). Ernst Pepping (1901–1981) was a church musician who, after the war, became professor of composition at the University of Music in Berlin.

rary music" is due to the fact that it is precisely "the 'denial' of beauty in the strict union of music to the word of God," that makes their "achievement true and great."[9]

If this is so, then Hanfried Müller's later claim that Bonhoeffer found himself theologically on the "wrong track" during the time he wrote *Discipleship* and *Life Together*,[10] also finds some support from a musical perspective. Indeed, it is indisputable that there is a certain similarity between Bonhoeffer's position and what Theodor W. Adorno described as a musical "traditionalism," which renders homage to "a cult of the past perfect." As Adorno explains, "One abdicates from . . . contact with the only tradition that extends into the childhood of those living today . . . It is the musical world of the parents. Musical traditionalism taboos the 19th century . . . on account of very poor reasons like that of the alleged overcoming of Romanticism."[11] Should we, then, regard Bonhoeffer as a *ressentiment-listener* fixated on a collective that is structured in an authoritarian way, as Adorno's theory might suggest? As Adorno writes, the type of *ressentiment-listener* is represented by

> these so-called Bach-lovers, against whom I have defended Bach, and even more by those who are fixated with pre-Bachian music . . . The *ressentiment-listener* in protesting against the commercialization of music in an apparently nonconformist way, sympathizes with the orders and collectives for their own sake, with all the sociopsychological and political consequences . . . And he cannot tolerate the thought of subjective expression which is, for him, profoundly the same as promiscuity.[12]

If this is the case then it presents certain difficulties, because Bonhoeffer's *ressentiment* is not directed against the "new music" of that period, such as that of the Second Vienna School (Schönberg et al.) or of Stravinsky, of which he was probably not even yet

9. Bonhoeffer, *Conspiracy and Imprisonment*, 39.

10. See Müller, *Von der Kirche zur Welt*, 252.

11. See Adorno, "Tradition," in *Dissonanzen*. 137.

12. See Adorno, Einleitung in die Musiksoziologie (1962/68; author's translation).

aware. This lack of knowledge may be explained by the taboo imposed by the Nazis on "degenerate" art, a taboo largely supported in church circles, as confirmed by Bonhoeffer's preference for church composers like Distler and Pepping. The exclusion of such music from Bonhoeffer's consciousness as a member of the educated bourgeoisie (*Bildungsbürgertum*) parallels the simultaneous ignorance of the "Jewish renaissance" (Buber, Rosenzweig, and so forth) and of the critical social research of the Frankfurt School, which included Adorno, the foremost musical theorist.

Given this, Bonhoeffer's *ressentiment* is directed rather against "contemporaries" like Richard Strauss and Hans Pfitzner, whose modernity consisted essentially in an epicurean exaggeration of the musical tradition of the nineteenth century. This tradition was incapable of offering any resistance to Nazi authoritarian demands. Admittedly, Bonhoeffer's objection to this late bourgeois music tradition would, then, also apply to Beethoven's desire for autonomy.[13] But his objection is especially aimed at a bourgeoisie that had already given up on autonomy long ago. What should also be noted is that Bonhoeffer's antiromantic *ressentiment* remains limited to the realm of the church. Outside that realm, Bonhoeffer did not play down his romantic heritage but, as during his Finkenwalde period, deliberately cultivated it.[14] But this then raises questions about the strict partitioning of music into a sacred and a worldly realm, a separation that, in any case, would later be subjected to Bonhoeffer's critique of "thinking in two spheres."[15]

But we also need to question whether the term *ressentiment*, which refers to a spontaneous dislike, correctly describes Bonhoeffer's theological and sociological opposition to the bourgeois music tradition of the nineteenth century. Rather we should say that Bonhoeffer's attitude is partly justified by his observation that those educated in the classical-romantic music tradition were

13. See Bonhoeffer's disappointment about Beethoven's *Creatures of Prometheus* (January 25,1941) in Bonhoeffer, *Conspiracy and Imprisonment*, 128.

14. Bethge, *Dietrich Bonhoeffer*, 429.

15. See Bonhoeffer, *Ethics*, 55. Bonhoeffer, *Letters and Papers from Prison*, 478–80;

especially vulnerable to Nazi propaganda. This is supported by the memory of his fellow Tegel prisoner Gaetano Latmiral that, according to Bonhoeffer, "the Nazis had a fanatically tragic will to involve everyone in the catastrophe," and that for him "Wagner's music was an expression of this barbarous pagan psychology."[16] In the light of such antipagan sentiments, it would be better to concede a certain "historical necessity" to Bonhoeffer's bias towards "traditionalism" rather than regarding it as a "wrong track."

What is eventually significant is, that Bonhoeffer's (let's call it!) "authoritarian" fixation during the Finkenwalde period, which is apparent in the way he wants to "bind" music to the church, is qualified Christologically. For him the "binding" of music is primarily a binding to Jesus Christ as Lord of the church.[17] In other words, the theological reason for Bonhoeffer's suspicion towards all "outer appearance" in this unreconciled world lies in the Christological claim that the servant of God, according to Isaiah 53, has "no form or beauty."[18] In contrast to Augustine, who states that "truth shines through beauty," Bonhoeffer was, in this respect, an unconscious follower of Schönberg's postulate: "music should not ornament, but be true."[19]

As we shall see later, this Christological qualification of Bonhoeffer's reservation finally breaks open new possibilities for musical appreciation. On the one hand, we gain a critical authority with respect to the danger of a musical clericalism, for being bound to Christ can, at times also signify opposition to the church. On the other hand, for music to be bound to Jesus Christ can also mean a relative rehabilitation of the "natural" and of passion in music.

---

16. See Bethge, *Dietrich Bonhoeffer*, 851.

17. See Bonhoeffer, *Conspiracy and Imprisonment:* 38–39, where Bonhoeffer speaks about the abnegation of beauty "for Christ's sake" and about the "strong binding of music to the Word of God" and not to the authority of the church.

18. See Bonhoeffer, *Letters and Papers from Prison*, 480.

19. Quoted according to Adorno, *Philosophie der neuen Musik*, 46.

Being bound to Christ would then also manifest itself in music as "being set free to live in genuine worldliness."[20]

Both possibilities made a noticeable impact on Bonhoeffer during his imprisonment. He experienced the conspiracy against Hitler and his imprisonment as an intensification of commitment to Christ, but at the same time as a certain distancing from the church that refused to join him on this path.[21] In addition, the surprising experience of solidarity in the Resistance between Christians and humanists, who were alienated from the church, had its musical equivalent, namely, in the acknowledgment of Bach, not only as a church composer, but also as a "worldly" composer,[22] as well as in a new appreciation for the late Beethoven.[23]

20. Bonhoeffer, *Ethics*, 400.

21. See Bethge, *Dietrich Bonhoeffer*, 794. "After he had been connected with the 'conspiracy' Bonhoeffer assumed that his church would no longer be able to use him . . ."

22. See Bonhoeffer, *Letters and Papers from Prison*, 306.

23. See Bonhoeffer, *Letters and Papers from Prison*, 332.

3

The Lutheran Chorales

IF BONHOEFFER'S CHRISTOLOGICAL CONCENTRATION during the Finkenwalde period created the danger of a clerical or churchly narrowing, and a *ressentiment* against the classical-romantic musical tradition, such concentration forms the background of Bonhoeffer's "worldly" understanding of music that developed during his imprisonment. In prison the *Lutheran chorales*, especially those with words written by Paul Gerhardt, which he often quoted, offered Bonhoeffer support.[1]

For Bonhoeffer, the church struggle during the thirties triggered an intense debate about the traditional role of hymns as an expression of the "inner life" within the Protestant church. During the Berlin Olympic Games in 1936, Bonhoeffer gave a lecture[2] in

1. See Bonhoeffer, *Letters and Papers from Prison*, 56, 78, 104, 179, 196, 220, 230, 242.

2. The lecture on "The Inner Life of the German Evangelical Church" was given as part of a series organized by the Confessing Church during the Olympics on August 5th, 1936, in Apostle Paul's Church in Berlin-Schöneberg. It is quoted here from notes made by one of Bonhoeffer's students in Finkenwalde, Gerhard Riemer. Bonhoeffer wrote to Bethge while he was working

which he interpreted Christian hymn singing as a sign of protest by default against the rule of state power: "The ancient Christians were still singing even as they were being thrown to the lions."[3] However, for him, Gerhardt's songs no longer seemed to bear testimony "to the great struggles of faith of early Christendom"[4] and of the Reformation. "The emphasis in Paul Gerhardt is that I have Christ. I can put my trust in him. Hence it is no longer between heaven and hell that the battle rages; I myself am the battleground."[5] In concluding his lecture Bonhoeffer said that it probably was not a coincidence that the church struggle led to the emergence of new hymns in the spirit of the Reformation.[6] "We are not allowed to look back except to the cross of Christ. Nor are we allowed to look into the future except to the Last Judgment. And so we have been made free to praise and to sing!"[7]

In prison it is especially the *lyrics* of the songs that take on great significance for Bonhoeffer; through them the melodies are "bound to the Word."[8] His preference for Paul Gerhardt's lyrics indicate a certain loosening of the rigid battle position of 1936. Back then he had accused the Gerhardt hymns of being responsible for the way the Reformation's battle of faith had withdrawn into inwardness. But now, in prison, Bonhoeffer even acquires a taste

---

on this lecture on July 31, 1936: "I am meddling in your craft, and I will be doing it using hymns from Luther, Gerhardt, Zinzendorf, Gellert; I'm not yet sure what other material. It is not easy. You could perhaps do a better job." Zinzendorf's texts even "embarrass" him (Bonhoeffer, *Theological Education at Finkenwalde,* 227).

3. Bonhoeffer, *Theological Education at Finkenwalde,* 710.

4. Bonhoeffer, *Theological Education at Finkenwalde,* 712.

5. Bonhoeffer, *London,* 713.

6. In this connection, to the surprise of a reporter from *Die Christliche Welt* (cf. *Theological Education at Finkenwalde* 717 n. 38), Bonhoeffer is thinking of the songs of Heinrich Vogel.

7. Bonhoeffer, *Theological Education at Finkenwalde,* 717.

8. See the reference to *Neues Lied* No. 370, 3–4 (*Evangelisches Gesangbuch,* Nr. 283) in Bonhoeffer's letter to Bethge dated August 28, 1944; those verses read *inter alia* "O may God grant us / an end to war, an end to weapons . . ." (Bonhoeffer, *Letters and Papers from Prison,* 493 n. 14).

for the monastic mysticism of the Christmas song "I Stand beside Your Manger Here."[9] On August 4, 1943,[10] he writes to Bethge:

> Probably one has to be alone a long time and read it meditatively in order to be able to take it in. Every word is extraordinarily replete and radiant. It's just a little monastic-mystical, yet only as much as is warranted, for alongside the "we" there is indeed also an "I and Christ."[11]

We notice here an obvious intensification of being bound to Christ, or an "internalization" of faith; this should not be understood as inward withdrawal, but rather as a response to the challenge posed by the solitude of imprisonment.

Again, on the first Sunday of Advent that same year, Bonhoeffer quotes alongside the lyrics also the Advent melody of the hymn "Saviour of the Nations Come,"[12] Martin Luther's adaptation of an early church hymn by Ambrose of Milan. The quotation relates to the fourth verse ("Now your manger, shining bright . . .)[13] and its eight notes making up the beginning and ending motif of the melody:

In this regard, Bonhoeffer attaches importance to this melody being sung "not in 4/4 meter, rather in the suspended, anticipatory rhythm that corresponds to the text!"[14] Thus Bonhoeffer tries to avoid the isometry aspired to in Luther's hymns, which—like the militaristically abused "A Mighty Fortress"[15]—can grow into an assertive march rhythm. Instead, Bonhoeffer reaches back to the

9. See *Evangelical Lutheran Hymnbook,* no. 129. Bonhoeffer, *Letters and Papers from Prison,* 230 fn. 20.

10. See Bonhoeffer, *Letters and Papers from Prison,* 249 fn. 14.

11. Bonhoeffer, *Letters and Papers from Prison,* 230.

12. See *Evangelical Lutheran Hymnbook,* no. 263.

13. Bonhoeffer, *Letters and Papers from Prison,* 202.

14. Bonhoeffer, *Letters and Papers from Prison,* 202.

15. *Ein' feste Burg*—the most influential hymn of the Lutheran Reformation.

rhythmically looser Gregorian practice of chanting in the early and medieval church, which would be appropriate for the hymns of Ambrose of Milan. One can look at it as the musical counterpart to Bonhoeffer's comment in the letter of the previous week, according to which the church fathers appear to him "to some extent much more contemporaneous than the Reformers."[16]

16. Bonhoeffer, *Letters and Papers from Prison*, 189.

4

Heinrich Schütz and the "Recapitulation of All Things"

THE MUSICAL AUTHORITY BONHOEFFER quoted most during his imprisonment was Heinrich Schütz. Bethge had introduced Bonhoeffer to Schütz's work when they were at the Finkenwalde seminary. In a letter dated the 4th February 1941, written from the Benedictine monastery in Ettal, Bonhoeffer thanked Bethge for sending him Hans Joachim Moser's biography of Schütz for his birthday.[1] In doing so he wrote:

> I am indebted to you for H. Schütz and with him for a whole rich world. Gladly I would accompany you on "Eile, mich, Gott, zu erretten,"[2] which I have been humming to myself again with the attached sheet music. And I believe it is no coincidence that Schütz came to me through none other than you.[3]

1. Bonhoeffer, *Conspiracy and Imprisonment,* 134. Moser, *Heinrich Schütz.*
2. "Make haste, O God, to deliver me" (Ps 70 v. 1).
3. Bonhoeffer, *Conspiracy and Imprisonment* 139.

Like the chorales, so Schütz's compositions also became significant for Bonhoeffer in prison, largely because of the lyrics. Once again, from Bonhoeffer's perspective, a firm connection with the Word seems to determine the musical value of the compositions. Several times in his prison letters, in addition to Psalms 3 and 47,[4] he quotes Psalm 70 ("Make haste, O God, to deliver me") according to Schütz's scoring.[5] This selection of psalms provides a glimpse into Bonhoeffer's own practice of prayer, as reflected in the Psalter. What "alone is important," he writes in *The Prayer book of the Bible*, "is that we begin anew with confidence and love to pray the Psalms in the name of our Lord Jesus Christ."[6] In the prison letters we hear his plea for help against his enemies (Psalms 3 and 70), as well as his hope that God would show his awesomeness to the Gentiles through his choice of "the pride of Jacob whom he loves" (Psalm 47).[7]

We could also explain the relevance that Bethge and Bonhoeffer, together with many others during the war, attributed to the *Kleine Geistliche Konzerte* of Schütz, not least because of the

4. Regarding Psalm 3 (vv. 5–9) cf. Schütz, *Anderer Theil Kleinen Geistlichen Concerten*, no. 5: "Ich liege und schlafe . . ." [I lie down and sleep] (Schütz Werke Verzeichnis [SWV] 310 96ff. Regarding Psalm 47 cf. Schütz, *Symphoniae Sacrae Secunda Pars*, 82ff: "Frohlocket mit Händen . . ." (SWV 349). Bonhoeffer mentions both scorings in his letters from prison Bonhoeffer, *Letters and Papers from Prison*, 81, 398, 398 n. 23, 87. Bonhoeffer also mentions the "Kleine Geistliche Konzert" on Psalm 27:4 "One thing I ask of the Lord . . ." in: Schütz, *Erster Theil Kleiner Geistlichen Concerten*, no. 13 100ff.; cf. Bonhoeffer, *Letters and Papers from Prison*, 231.

5. See Schütz, *Erster Theil Kleiner Geistlichen Concerten*, no. 1 Bonhoeffer mentions this "Geistliche Konzert" four times in his letters from prison. Bonhoeffer, *Letters and Papers from Prison*, 81 (with n. 20), 187 (with n. 50), 231 (with n. 27), 398 (with n. 23).

6. Bonhoeffer, *Life Together: Prayerbook of the Bible*, 177.

7. In a letter to Pangritz, dated 12th September 1984, Bethge points out that the "selection" of Psalm texts, which Bonhoeffer remembers in Schütz's scoring, also had to do with what was commercially available at the time. "Bärenreiter is also part of the encounter with Schütz. Wherever we went into a store, we checked for their editions, which had appeared and which seemed to us technically performable." SWV 282 and 285 were republished in 1936 by Hans Hoffmann.

similar situation in which they were composed during the Thirty Year's War: "The *Kleine Geistliche Konzerte* are Heinrich Schütz's musical 'Nevertheless' in the face of the war and the consequences of war."[8] Bonhoeffer can no longer read these psalms "without hearing them in the musical settings by Heinrich Schütz,"[9] where the words of the psalm are interpreted and accentuated with the help of musical tropes. Telling examples are the strongly jagged figure, "you break the teeth of the wicked" in Psalm 3; the threefold repetition of the mocking "Aha!" of the enemies (Ps 70:4); the expressive ascent of the melodic line all the way to g' on "mein Gott, verzeuch nicht [O Lord, do not delay]" (Ps 70:6), but also the artful scoring of the significantly mysterious Selah in Pss 3 and 47.

On one occasion, in a letter to Bethge on the fourth Sunday in Advent 1943, Bonhoeffer quotes the score of a *Geistliches Konzert*. In this instance it does not refer to the musical arrangement of a psalm, but to the German version of an Augustinian hymn on Christ, by Schütz: "O süßer, o freundlicher, o gütiger Herr Jesu Christe . . ." [O sweet, o kindly, o good Lord Jesus Christ].[10] Bonhoeffer refers to the ascending figure of seven notes, which is repeated four times on the "O" in the passage "O how my soul longs for you." At the same time, there is, in the music, an

8. Brodde, *Heinrich Schütz*, 149. Cf. Schütz's dedication of the first volume of his "Kleine Geistliche Konzerte" (1636): "It is obvious for many observers, in which way the laudable music among other liberal arts has severely declined and at some places even been destroyed by the ongoing dangerous events of war in our beloved fatherland of German nation." Cf. also the dedication of the second volume (1639): "I am ashamed to appear in the face of His Serenity with such small and simple works. But the wickedness of the present times is unfavorable for the liberal arts and does not permit my other works, which I have at hand without any glory, to appear in public. At the moment there was no other choice, therefore, than this poor work. But should the arts, which have nearly been suffocated and trodden into the mud by the arms now, be elevated again to their former dignity and value by the mercy of God, I will not forget to appear according to my duty in the face of His Princely Serenity with a richer pledge." Quoted by Wilhelm Ehmann, Vorwort, in: Schütz, *Neue Ausgabe sämtlicher Werke*, 10:vii.

9. Bonhoeffer, *Letters and Papers from Prison*, 81.

10. Bonhoeffer, *Letters and Papers from Prison*, 231. See Schütz, *Erster Theil Kleiner Geistlichen Concerten*, 83ff.

extraordinary intensification of expression through the sequencing ascent within the circle of fifths (e flat–b flat, b flat–f, f–c, c–g). Moser highlights how, merely through the temporal stretch of the musical trope, the "ecstatic expression of yearning" in the hymn becomes the "centre and climax" of Schütz's work. Quite rightly, Moser points out the relation of this trope to the melodic "O" in Schütz's *Song of Songs* motet "O, quam tu pulchra es . . ."[11] For without doubt the language of Augustine's hymn is also erotically charged. "My helper, with your love you have taken my heart, so that I long for you incessantly . . ." Bonhoeffer then comments with a clear allusion to Moser's formulation: "I also occasionally think of the o ————————! from the Augustinian 'O bone Jesu,' by Schütz.

In a certain way, namely, in its devotion—ecstatic, aching, and nevertheless so pure—isn't this passage something like the 'restoration' of all earthly desire?"[12] We already have here, in musical terms, Bonhoeffer's Christological concentration, even before his theological question, "who is Christ really for us today?"[13] gains its full intensity and intimacy. Considering that only a few lines before that, Bonhoeffer has also quoted the hymn "I Stand beside Your Manger Here," which he experiences as "just a little monastic-mystical,"[14] we might even speak of a tendency towards a Christ-mysticism. But we need to bear in mind that after mentioning Schütz's ecstatic "O," Bonhoeffer continues austerely: "By the way, 'restoration' is, of course, not to be confused with 'sublimation'!"[15]

11. See Moser, *Heinrich Schütz,* 436–37. Cf. Schütz, "O quam tu pulchra es, amica mea / Veni de Libano, amica mea" (double motet, SWV 265/66), in: *Symphoniae Sacrae. Neue Ausgabe sämtlicher Werke,* 13:72ff.

12. Bonhoeffer, *Letters and Papers from Prison,* 230–31.

13. Bonhoeffer, *Letters and Papers from Prison,* 362.

14. Bonhoeffer, *Letters and Papers from Prison,* 230.

15. Bonhoeffer, *Letters and Papers from Prison,* 231.

In fact, the *recapitulation of all things* is the theme to which the whole section is devoted. What, then, is Bonhoeffer's concern?

What gives rise to his train of thought is, once again, a verse by Paul Gerhardt, the fifth stanza from the Christmas hymn "Fröhlich soll mein Herze springen" [All my heart this night rejoices]. Bonhoeffer writes:

> In recent weeks this line has been running through my head over and over: "Calm your hearts, dear friends; / whatever plagues you, / whatever fails you, / I will restore it all." What does that mean, "I will restore it all"? Nothing is lost; in Christ all things are taken up, preserved, albeit in transfigured form, transparent, clear, liberated from the torment of self-serving demands. Christ brings all this back, indeed, as God intended, without being distorted by sin.[16]

Bonhoeffer alludes here to Irenaeus of Lyon's "doctrine of the restoration of all things" (recapitulation), which he experiences as a "consummately consoling thought."[17] The idea appears to him as the appropriate theological answer to the "longing for something past," which overtakes him "at completely unpredictable times."[18] "In my experience," he writes, "there is no greater torment than longing . . . and in the months here in prison I have had a quite terrible longing a couple of times."[19] He will under no circumstances be satisfied with a substitute for what is lost and missed. He writes:

> The substitute repulses us. We simply have to wait and wait; we have to suffer indescribably from the separation;

16. Bonhoeffer, *Letters and Papers from Prison*, 229–30.

17. Bonhoeffer, *Letters and Papers from Prison*, 230. See Irenaeus, *Adversus haereses*: I.10.1 (in the *regula fidei*): We believe "in the one Jesus Christ . . . and His coming from heaven in the glory of the Father to recapitulate all things [ἐπὶ τὸ ἀνακεφαλαιώσασθαι τὰ πάντα], and to raise up all flesh of the whole human race . . ." (Irenaeus, *Against the Heresies*, 55]). Irenaeus has Eph 1:10 in mind: "that in the dispensation of the fulfilment of the times he might restore all things by the Christ, both those which are in heaven and those which are on earth" (JB).

18. Bonhoeffer, *Letters and Papers from Prison*, 229.

19. Bonhoeffer, *Letters and Papers from Prison*, 227.

> we have to experience longing practically to the point of
> becoming ill—and only in this way do we sustain com-
> munion with the people we love, even if in a very painful
> way . . . Further, there is nothing more mistaken than to
> attempt to acquire for oneself in such times some sort of
> substitute for what is unattainable.[20]

Instead of substitutes, Bonhoeffer seeks "the power to overcome the tension," by fully concentrating on "the object of one's longing."[21] And he is convinced that Christ will bring back all of this, "indeed, as God intended, without being distorted by sin."[22]

Bonhoeffer, it seems, understands the teaching of Irenaeus about the *recapitulatio* (ἀνακεφαλαίωσις) from a historical or per- haps an end-time perspective, that is, as the eschatological "res- toration of all things" through the one who has "come again." In this regard he deviates distinctly from the dominant theological school of thought, according to which it is about the cosmological- gnostic "summing up" of all things in Christ.[23]

There is a striking parallel in Walter Benjamin with regard to this historical understanding of the notion of *recapitulatio*, which made the musical association with the longing "O" of Schütz pos- sible in the first place. By the time Bonhoeffer had written his letter to Bethge, Benjamin had already taken his own life on the French- Spanish border while trying to escape from Nazi henchmen. In his last, posthumously published text, "Über den Begriff der Geschichte" [On the concept of history] (1940), Benjamin writes

---

20. Bonhoeffer, *Letters and Papers from Prison*, 227–28.

21. Bonhoeffer, *Letters and Papers from Prison*, 228.

22. Bonhoeffer, *Letters and Papers from Prison*, 230. With regard to the notion of 'restoration' or 'bringing back' (*Wiederbringung*) in Bonhoeffer's thought cf. the discussion between Barth and Bonhoeffer in 1941, conveyed by Jørgen Glenthøj: "Bonhoeffer asks: Do you believe that everything will come back (*wiederkommen*)? Will it be—like Lake Geneva? Karl Barth: Yes, like Lake Geneva" Glenthøj, "Bonhoeffer und die Ökumene," 198

23. See for example Scharl, *Recapitulatio mundi*; cf. also Luther's gloss in relation to his translation of Eph 1:10 ("zusammengefaßt" [summed up]): "God wants that everything be subject to Christ and that he be acknowledged as Lord and head."

about the "messianic time," that it "sums up (*zusammenfaßt*) the history of all humanity in one tremendous instant." Here "summing up" means "bringing back again," for it concerns the perception of "a revolutionary chance in the fight for the oppressed past."[24] The background to Benjamin's thinking is the kabbalistic teaching of the Messianic *Tikkun* as "the restoration of the harmonious state of the world."[25]

This historization of the idea of *recapitulatio* in the sense of a "restoration" of what is lost is strongly supported in the Hebrew Bible. As a matter of fact, Bonhoeffer interprets the recapitulation or ἀνακεφαλαίωσις of Eph 1:10, not in terms of the gnostic redeemer myth, but biblically against the backdrop of Ecclesiastes 3, which says: "God seeks out what has gone by" (v. 15)[26] Bonhoeffer comments: "nothing of the past is lost, that God seeks out with us the past that belongs to us to reclaim it."[27] This Old Testament insight thus finds its Christological fulfillment in the Letter to the Ephesians and the teaching of Irenaeus. And no one managed to "express this with such simplicity and childlikeness as Paul Gerhardt in the words he places in the Christ child's mouth: 'I will restore it all.'"[28]

But in what ways does such an understanding of "bringing back again" really avoid the danger of a "sublimation"? In as far as sublimation represents the attempt to satisfy the desire for what one is deprived of through a substitute or an act of spiritualization,

24. Benjamin, "Über den Begriff der Geschichte," 702–3.

25. See Scholem, "Zum Verständnis der messianischen Idee im Judentum," 30.

26. Martin Buber translates it in an even more dramatic way: "Das Verjagte, Gott suchts hervor" [What is chased away, God looks for]. The combination of Eccl 3:15 with Eph 1:10 can apparently be found already in Irenaeus. See Grillmeier, *Christ in the Christian Tradition*, 1:101–4. See also Irenaeus *Adversus haereses* V.14.2: "Flesh and blood possessed what had been lost . . . Consequently, he too had flesh and blood when he sought out what was lost and in himself . . . recapitulated the Father's primordial creation." Here Irenaeus's *recapitulatio* means "bringing back again" (restoration) rather than "summing up." See Bonhoeffer, *Letters and Papers from Prison*, 230, fn. 17.

27. Bonhoeffer, *Letters and Papers from Prison*, 229.

28. Bonhoeffer, *Letters and Papers from Prison*, 230.

Bonhoeffer refers to it as "flesh." By contrast, true recapitulation can only be thought of as "a new creation" through the "Holy Spirit": "'Sublimation' is σάρξ, (and pietistic?!), whereas 'restoration' is spirit, meant not in the sense of 'spiritualization' (which is also σάρξ) but of καινή κτίσις (a 'new creation') through the πνεῦμα ἅγιον (Holy Spirit)."[29] While simultaneously rejecting a pious compensatory satisfaction Bonhoeffer gives expression to the expectation of a new creation by putting the emphasis in the sentence "*I* will restore it all"—on the first word, "I"—"that means we cannot and should not take it back again ourselves but allow ourselves to be given it by Christ."[30] Since this is especially true in the relationship between the living and the dead, Bonhoeffer expresses the wish, that Schütz's work "O bone Jesu" be sung at his funeral.[31] According to his understanding, this genuinely expressed the "restoration" of all earthly desire through Christ.

Besides this, there is also a remarkable parallel between Benjamin's text and Bonhoeffer's resistance to false comfort through a spiritualized stilling of desire (i.e., one that is at the same time a stilling that is arbitrary in its anticipation). In Benjamin's essay "On the Concept of History" we also find the prohibition to arbitrarily rule over the restitution of what is lost, or rather, to overplay the desire with a cheap substitute. The prohibition is mentioned there under the concept of *Eingedenken* (remembrance): "As is well-known, Jews were prohibited from speculating about the future. Instead, Torah and prayer instruct them to remember. Judaism demystified the future, but those who succumbed to such

---

29. Bonhoeffer, *Letters and Papers from Prison*, 231. Cf. Bonhoeffer's appreciation of Barth's criticism of religion in his letter to Bethge of 8 June 1944: "He led the God of Jesus Christ forward to battle against religion, πνεῦμα against σάρξ. That remains his greatest merit" (Bonhoeffer, *Letters and Papers from Prison*, 429). Bonhoeffer's understanding of 'recapitulation' as a new creation through the Holy Spirit indicates that he perceives also Barth's slogan "πνεῦμα against σάρξ" in terms of biblical materialism instead of idealistic spiritualization.

30. Bonhoeffer, *Letters and Papers from Prison*, 231.

31. In addition, he requests Psalms 27 and 70. Bonhoeffer, *Letters and Papers from Prison*, 231.

speculation went to soothsayers for their enlightenment. But this did not mean that for Jews the future had become homogenous and empty. For at any moment the Messiah could enter through the narrow gate."[32]

In the end, however, Bonhoeffer's preference for Schütz at this point has little to do with a *ressentiment* towards the romantic music tradition. This is shown by the fact that on 30th May 1944, after more than a year of imprisonment, "Solvejg's Song" from *Peer Gynt* by Edvard Grieg, which Bonhoeffer heard on the radio, could now suddenly fulfil a very similar function to Schütz's "O bone Jesu" half a year before in view of the problem of the transience of life and Bonhoeffer's longing for the outside world. Grieg's song has, as he confesses in a letter to Bethge,

> really moved me. To wait faithfully an entire lifetime—
> that is the triumph over the hostility of space, that is,
> over separation, and time, that is, over transience. Don't
> you think that such faithfulness alone makes one happy,
> and unfaithfulness unhappy?[33]

Without doubt, the rare opportunity of listening to music on the radio was already an exhilarating experience for an inmate who otherwise had to endure very different noises. Earlier he had written: "I sometimes have actual hunger for an evening of trios, quartets, or singing. Once in a while, my ears would really like to hear something other than the voices in this building."[34] And, later, he writes: "it's bizarre when announcements like 'enemy air squadrons approaching . . .' break right into the music. The connection between the two isn't that immediately obvious."[35]

It should be added however, that "Solvejg's Song" does not represent some random piece; rather its lyrics express a topic which

32. Benjamin, "Über den Begriff der Geschichte," 704.

33. Bonhoeffer, *Letters and Papers from Prison*, 407–8.

34. Bonhoeffer, *Letters and Papers from Prison*, 176.

35. Bonhoeffer, *Letters and Papers from Prison*, 375. See also the poem "Night Voices" in Bonhoeffer, *Letters and Papers from Prison*, 462–70.

had occupied Bonhoeffer intensely: faithfulness to "the past."[36] In a letter to Bethge on June 4th, 1944, he writes:

> For me, this confrontation with the past, this attempt to hold on to it and to get it back, and above all the fear of losing it, is almost the daily background music of my life here, which at times—especially after brief visits, which are always followed by long partings—becomes a theme with variations.[37]

On long, warm May evenings he feels the need to move out, "and one could do crazy things if one weren't so 'sensible.' Could one perhaps have become *too* sensible already?" In any case, using rather carefree words, Bonhoeffer talks about how much effort it takes him, "after such a long time of deliberately beating back every desire one has" until "things all build up until one day there's a terrible explosion." He almost fears self-tormenting daydreams and so escapes "into thinking, writing letters, being glad about your happiness."[38] In this way Bonhoeffer tries to overcome the animosity of space and time by remaining faithful to what he is deprived of, while at the same time—as self-protection—prohibiting his own desire: "Paradoxical though it may sound, it would be more selfless if I didn't need to fear my desire but could give it free rein—but that's very hard."[39] In this situation "Solvejg's Song" is like a fuse at a powder keg.

---

36. Here, the text of Solveig's song should be taken in account: "Perhaps there will go both winter and spring, / And next summer also and the whole year, / But onetime you will come, I know this for sure, / And I shall surely wait for I promised that last. // God strengthen you where you go in the world, / God give you joy if you before his footstool stand, / Here shall I wait until you come again, / And if you wait above, we'll meet there again, my friend!" (https://lyricstranslate.com/de/solvejgs-song-solveigs-song.html, retrieved 10 March, 2019).

37. Bonhoeffer, *Letters and Papers from Prison*, 416: See also Bonhoeffer's poem "The Past" in Bonhoeffer, *Letters and Papers from Prison*, 418–21, a memorial to his friendship with Bethge and, at the same time, a love poem for his fiancée Maria von Wedemeyer. Bonhoeffer and von Wedemeyer, *Love Letters from Cell 92*, 210–13.

38. Bonhoeffer, *Letters and Papers from Prison*, 407.

39. Bonhoeffer, *Letters and Papers from Prison*, 407.

In this respect it certainly corresponds with his own experience, when, meditating in the Advent letter on the "bringing back again" of what is lost in relation to Schütz's "O bone Jesu," Bonhoeffer feels at the same time that he must point out a "danger" in music. This applies to the case of the "sweet old man," who every year comes to prison to play Christmas carols on his trumpet with the result that "the prisoners wail in misery."[40] Bonhoeffer thinks

> that in the face of *this* misery that reigns in this building, a remembrance of Christmas that is merely more or less only playfully sentimental is inappropriate. A good, personal word, a sermon, should accompany it. Without that, music on its own can in fact become dangerous.[41]

A playful-sentimental remembering of the past without the accompaniment of critical reflection represents at best a substitute gratification. It cannot keep alive the faithfulness to what is lacking, let alone recover what has been lost. Clearly this is also felt by the inmates who have been "demoralised" by the Christmas carols. Which is why in "previous years . . . the prisoners repeatedly whistled and made lots of noise while he was playing, simply in order not to weaken,"[42] or, because they would not allow themselves to be put off so cheaply. The desire for what is lacking should not be covered up by a sentimental substitute. Faithfulness to what is lost demands that the tension of deprivation is endured. Or, with the words of the philosopher Ernst Bloch: "Music begins wistfully and by all means as a cry for what is lacking."[43]

40. Bonhoeffer, *Letters and Papers from Prison*, 232.
41. Bonhoeffer, *Letters and Papers from Prison*, 232.
42. Bonhoeffer, *Letters and Papers from Prison*, 232.
43. Bloch, *Das Prinzip Hoffnung*, 1244.

5

The Art of Fugue and the Conspiracy

Bonhoeffer's opinion, according to which music is qualified by its "strict union . . . to the word of God,"[1] implies that without such bond with the preached word music may become dangerous. But in his prison letters he gives music a more positive role, something previously only foreshadowed. Now, music is given an unexpected freedom exactly because of its being anchored in Christology. Bonhoeffer is even prepared to make a significant correction to his doctrine of the mandates, which he wrote about in his *Ethics*. This can be seen in his letter of 23 January 1944 to Renate and Eberhard Bethge: "Who in our time could, for example, lightheartedly make music, nurture friendship, play, and be happy? Certainly not the 'ethical' person, but only the Christian."[2] How are we to understand this?

In an insertion (probably made during 1941) for an outline to his *Ethics* from the previous year ("Christ, Reality, and Good") Bonhoeffer still tried to concretize the "relationship of the Word to

1. Bonhoeffer, *Conspiracy and Imprisonment*, 39.
2. Bonhoeffer, *Letters and Papers from Prison*, 268.

Christ" through the four mandates: work, marriage, government and the church.[3] Music, a "foretaste of heavenly music" on earth, was regarded as Cain's creation under the mandate of work. "Cain's first creation was a city, the earthly reflection of the eternal city of God. Then followed the invention of violins and flutes, which give us on earth a foretaste of heavenly music."[4]

The concept of the doctrine of the mandates is rather fluid in Bonhoeffer. The mandate of work as discussed in "Christ, Reality and Good"[5] is later replaced by the mandate of culture in the draft "The Concrete Commandment and the Divine Mandates."[6] Bonhoeffer probably found the concept of work too narrow to subsume the arts within it. In a letter from prison on 23 January 1944 we come across the mandate of work again.[7] But now "culture and education (*Bildung*)" are no longer located in the "sphere of obedience," ordained by the mandates, but in the "sphere of freedom," that is, the space that makes creativity possible.[8] This occurs here for the first time and relativizes the mandates. Bonhoeffer no longer wants to subsume "culture and education" under work, "as tempting as that would be in many ways."[9] Along with friendship (about which he primarily reflects) music is seen, rather, as foundational to culture and education. And even though he still maintains that "marriage, work, state, and church each have their concrete divine mandates,"[10] what is entirely new when compared to his discussion in his *Ethics* is his reference to a "sphere of freedom" that encompasses this "sphere of obedience."[11]

---

3. Bonhoeffer, *Ethics*, 68.

4. Bonhoeffer, *Ethics*, 71.

5. Bonhoeffer, *Ethics*, 47–75.

6. Bonhoeffer, *Ethics*, 388–408. Probably spring 1943, see p. 388, notes 1 and 2.

7. Bonhoeffer, *Letters and Papers from Prison*, 267–68.

8. Bonhoeffer, *Letters and Papers from Prison*, 268 n. 23.

9. Bonhoeffer, *Letters and Papers from Prison*, 268.

10. Bonhoeffer, *Letters and Papers from Prison*, 267.

11. Bonhoeffer, *Letters and Papers from Prison*, 268.

At this stage Bonhoeffer does not seem to be clear about how to anchor this "sphere of freedom" Christologically. At one point, evidently experimenting, he adds after "freedom" in brackets: "of the Christian person!?" On the one hand, the "sphere of freedom" seems to be tightly bound to the fourth mandate (church), in contrast to "our world, which is defined by the *first* three mandates." On the other hand, the sphere of freedom should embrace all four mandates.[12] What becomes clear here is to what extent Bonhoeffer's theological thinking finds itself in an experimental flow, especially in the context of exchanging letters.

Our full humanity requires more than the four mandates, through which our "Prussian world is so strongly defined . . . that the whole sphere of freedom has been pushed into the background." So, without claiming that music has the "*necessitas*" of a divine command, Bonhoeffer now places it under "the '*necessitas*' of *freedom*."[13] It is an essential part of our full humanity "like the corn flowers belong to the field of grain."[14]

Suspended between its "obligation to the Word" and its autonomy in the "playground of freedom"—this understanding of the place of music is apparent again a month later (23 February 1944) when, in a letter to Bethge, Bonhoeffer speaks about Bach's *Art of Fugue*: "After all, there are such things as fragments . . . , which remain meaningful for hundreds of years, because only God could perfect them, so they must remain fragments—I'm thinking, for example, of *The Art of Fugue*."[15] Bonhoeffer thinks about this in correlation with the social location of his generation: "The longer

12. Bonhoeffer, *Letters and Papers from Prison*, 267–68.

13. Bonhoeffer, *Letters and Papers from Prison*, 268.

14. Bonhoeffer, *Letters and Papers from Prison*, 269. See Bonhoeffer's poem "The Friend" in Bonhoeffer, *Letters and Papers from Prison*, 526–30.

15. Bonhoeffer, *Letters and Papers from Prison*, 306. In a letter to the author (12 August 1984), Eberhard Bethge remembered that he and Bonhoeffer "probably had a score of the *Art of Fugue* at that time." Mainly, however, they used the edition by Erich Schwebsch, an adaptation for two pianos, which they bought. By means of this edition they "time and again here and there" tried this work out practically, using "the virginal" they had acquired in 1938 "together with the grand piano."

we are uprooted from our real professional and personal lives, the more we experience our lives—in contrast to our parents' lives—as fragmented."[16] The time of the "universal scholar" and the "specialist," Bonhoeffer says, is over, "our intellectual existence remains but a torso . . . What matters," he continues, "is whether one still sees, in this fragment of life that we have, what the whole was intended and designed to be, and of what material it is made."[17]

It is not about the fragment according to the Romantic understanding of art, that is, as a freely chosen form in contrast to a closed system, but about the life of a whole generation for whom "the violence of outward events breaks our lives in pieces."[18] This is also made clear in a letter to Bethge with Bonhoeffer's reference to Jeremiah chapter 45 following his reflection on the correlation between *The Art of Fugue* and "our fragmented lives." "I can't get Jer. 45 out of my mind anymore," he writes, and continues by saying that the words "but I will give you your life as a prize of war," also refer "necessarily" to "a fragment of life."[19]

But to what extent can one speak, with regard to Bach's *Art of Fugue*, about a fragmentation brought about by social violence? After all, his work was shaped by a "scientific" approach influenced by the "universal scholarship" of that time. But we need to remember that the time of Bach's late and speculative work was also influenced by a "crisis of culture and of the Reformation," as Bach himself was well aware. "Bach," writes Ugo Duse, "must have

16. Bonhoeffer, *Letters and Papers from Prison*, 305. See also Bonhoeffer's letter to the parents from February 2, 1944, where he characterizes their life as "a balanced and fulfilled whole." In contrast he feels how "unfinished and fragmentary" the lives of his generation are. "But precisely that which is fragmentary may point to a higher fulfilment, which can no longer be achieved by human effort" (Bonhoeffer, *Letters and Papers from Prison*, 301).

17. Bonhoeffer, *Letters and Papers from Prison*, 306.

18. Bonhoeffer, *Letters and Papers from Prison*, 301.

19. Bonhoeffer, *Letters and Papers from Prison*, 306. See Jer 45:4–5 (ESV): "Thus says the Lord: Behold, what I have built I am breaking down, and what I have planted I am plucking up—that is, the whole land. And do you seek great things for yourself? Seek them not, for behold, I am bringing disaster upon all flesh, declares the Lord. But I will give you your life as a prize of war in all places to which you may go."

THE POLYPHONY OF LIFE

noticed the crisis in a much more varied way than we tend to think; he must have experienced it as a collective crisis of listening, as a crisis of social relations, as a crisis of familiar conditions, as a crisis of the old political despotism; and finally—in the face of Frederick the Great's unbiased politics of religion—he must have felt it as an enormous crisis of faith."[20] If, especially in *The Art of Fugue*, Bach was perceived as being conservative, then we need to keep in mind that "conservative in his day meant, *not* to be conservative." Bach's withdrawal into isolation can therefore be understood as a protest against the enlightened absolutism of Frederick II, which he would have experienced as a betrayal of the Reformation. At a time, when Frederick, the "liberal king," "had Jesuits as well as Protestant pastors hanged irrespectively, according to the same rule, when they called soldiers to desert," Bach made "the effort to a turn inwards, into self-isolation." In view of this, the social isolation of the late Bach is certainly comparable to the isolation of "modern music" that had already occurred "before the rise of Nazism."[21]

Thus, it does not seem arbitrary that Bonhoeffer, under the conditions of his imprisonment in a Nazi military prison, experiences the relevance of *The Art of Fugue* precisely because of its fragmentary character:

> If our life is only the most remote reflection of such a fragment, in which, even for a short time, the various themes gradually accumulate and harmonize with one another and in which great counterpoint is sustained from beginning to end—so that finally, when they cease, all one can do is intone the chorale "Vor Deinen Thron tret' ich allhier" [*sic*] instead of "hiermit"; Andreas Pangritz [Before your throne I now appear]—then it is

20. Duse, "Musik und Schweigen," 108 (translated by Robert Steiner).

21. Duse, "Musik und Schweigen," 111, 113, and 105. See in this respect the comment by Adorno in relation to the fragmentary character of Schönberg's and Berg's operas Adorno ("Einleitung in die Musiksoziologie," 260): "Evidently, in the present situation, everything of spiritual importance is doomed to be fragmentary" (author's translation).

not for us, either, to complain about this fragmentary life of ours, but rather even to be glad of it.[22]

Only two days before writing this, at the beginning of a letter on 21 February to Bethge, Bonhoeffer had written that he "often wondered here where we are to draw the line between necessary resistance [*Widerstand*] to 'fate' and equally necessary submission [*Ergebung*]."[23] He continued:

> Only on the *other side* of this twofold process can we speak of "being led." . . . So my question is basically . . . how "fate" really becomes "the state of being led."[24]

In other words, when God himself takes the resistance into his own hands, the human role is submission. Against this background, any false reconciliation by means of the closing chorale is excluded. Rather, it underlines, once again, that there can be no reconciliation with the powers of death, by pointing—beyond the handing over of our daily "penultimate" resistance into "ultimate" surrender—to the resistance that the living God himself initiates.

The music-historical question of how the chorale happened to be set at the end of *The Art of Fugue* does not seem to be of any interest to Bonhoeffer. We may note that in the preface of Erich Schwebsch's version, used by Bonhoeffer and Bethge, the restructuring of *The Art of Fugue* by Wolfgang Graeser is embellished by anthroposophy. The chorale does not appear to belong to the work, even though it is allowed to be a gesture of reconciliation at the end: "Without any external connection with the 'Art of Fugue,' in fact in a strange key, a melody is faintly heard, which was really meant to be expressed in the otherworldly greatness of the final harmony of the work, in fact of his whole life's work: 'Vor deinen Thron tret ich hiermit.'" And therefore, in spite of it all, the "added chorale is internally not unjustified." Rather, "in an unobtrusive form" it leads to a "reconciling return into the daily world, whose

---

22. Bonhoeffer, *Letters and Papers from Prison*, 306.

23. Bonhoeffer, *Letters and Papers from Prison*, 303.

24. Bonhoeffer, *Letters and Papers from Prison*, 304.

intrusion as a fall out of the greatest heights would have otherwise been experienced as unbearable."[25]

What is decisive for Bonhoeffer is the theological argument: If beyond the silence of the music, forced by the violence of death, "all one can do is intone the chorale,"[26] then this is a sign that the "fragment of our life" points to a "higher fulfilment that can no longer be achieved by human effort"[27] to a spirited resistance beyond surrender.[28] In a similar way Duse makes sense, not only of the abruption of *The Art of Fugue*, but also of the "possible resolution into the chorale," i.e., to point "beyond the sound." But this is already true about the abruption about which he comments: "In that way now the sound can no longer be to the higher glory of God; what remains, is the music of silence."[29]

Here we must note the interesting reference made by Winfried Maechler to the connection between *The Art of Fugue* and Bonhoeffer's participation in the political resistance against Hitler. According to Maechler, Bonhoeffer wrote to his friends on the war front about the progress of the resistance movement "as if it were preparations for a performance of *The Art of Fugue*, such as he had experienced in Berlin."[30] Maechler recalls: "I, myself, met him for the last time on holiday in Berlin. He was about to attend a performance of *The Art of Fugue* in the Charlottenburg Castle and promised to write to me sometime about the planned conspiracy [to assassinate Hitler], as though dealing with the performance of a concert. All I received was a single card, which said: 'Sadly the performance of the concert has been postponed, because some of the artists had to cancel.' Finally, when the performance was staged, it was too late."[31] So, for Bonhoeffer, it is probably no

25. Quoted according to Kolneder, *Die Kunst der Fuge*, 330 (translated by Robert Steiner).

26. Bonhoeffer, *Letters and Papers from Prison*, 306.

27. Bonhoeffer, *Letters and Papers from Prison*, 301.

28. Duse, "Musik und Schweigen," 112.

29. Duse, "Musik und Schweigen," 110 (translated by Robert Steiner).

30. Maechler, "Vom Pazifisten zum Widerstandskämpfer., 90).

31. Maechler, "Bonhoeffers Fanøer Friedenspredigt 104. The performance

coincidence that *The Art of Fugue* is comparable to the conspiracy plan, or that the attempted assassination is understood in terms of its performance.

Bonhoeffer understands the complex "free play" with the contrapuntal forms in Bach's last harpsichord work[32] as a reference to the "Word" in the chorale. In this way, he highlights the state of suspense in which the music now, according to him, finds itself: that is, between "being bound to the Word" as previously described, and liberation to "true worldliness" in the "sphere of freedom," which enfolds Christ and his commandment, that is, the world of mandates.[33] In this way he seems to move closer to Barth's understanding of music as fundamentally a "playing,"—something Barth came to realize, not so much through Bach, but rather through the music of Mozart: "our daily bread must also include playing . . . But play is something so lofty and demanding that it requires mastery. And in Mozart I hear the art of playing as I hear it in no one else."[34] This is also true in Mozart's church music, for Mozart

> did not really observe the well-established norm that the music should only serve the Word and explain it . . . But is that the only possible principle for church music? . . . If I hear him rightly, in his church music as in all his other creations, the music is a free counterpoint to that Word given to him. This is what inspires him, this is what he accompanies and plays about . . . In both he hears and respects the Word in its distinct form and character, but then to both he sets his own music—a music bound by the Word, but in this 'binding' still a sovereign shape with its own nature.[35]

attended by Bonhoeffer can only be that of Diener, who still presented the *Art of Fugue* in his version for string players several times during the war on the Day of Repentance and at the end of year in Berlin (cf. Kolneder, *Die Kunst der Fuge,*).

32. Cf. Leonhardt, *Art of Fugue*

33. Cf. Bonhoeffer, *Letters and Papers from Prison*, 268.

34. Barth, *Wolfgang Amadeus Mozart*, 16.

35. Barth, *Wolfgang Amadeus Mozart*, 38–39. We have used "Word" rather

With Bonhoeffer we would describe this music as "having come of age"!

In a letter to his parents on Repentance Day, 17 November 1943, Bonhoeffer was still occupied with the "spiritual" Bach, that is, those works bound to the Word already through their liturgical location: "For years," he writes, "Bach's B-minor Mass" belongs to this day, "just as the *St. Matthew Passion* is part of Good Friday."[36] In fact, Bonhoeffer describes the B-minor Mass as "Bach's most beautiful music," not least because it began with the great "Kyrie eleison," which, from the very moment he first heard it, made an "indescribable impression" on him, so much so that "everything else sank away completely,"[37] including his thoughts about his future career in theology. In a similar way, Wilhelm Dilthey had already "romanticized" this Kyrie by referring to it as "a superb example for the expression of divine infinity, which transcends the character of greatness itself, with the tools of polyphony . . . This expression contains more awareness of the religious movements in their ultimate depths, than would be accessible to any kind of reflection."[38]

How different are Bonhoeffer's reflections on *The Art of Fugue*! Bach's last work does not seem to drown everything else out but rather takes into itself all the "material" from which "our life" is built in order to process it anew, to play with it, and finally—as a fragment—to bring us to "the throne of the Most High." Maybe this indication of a "higher fulfilment that can no longer be achieved by human effort"[39] could then also include the hope of restoring what has been shattered. This could remind us of Walter Benjamin's meditation on the "angel of history": In the face of the "catastrophe, which incessantly piles debris upon debris and hurls

than "word" when the latter is used in this English translation.

36. Bonhoeffer, *Letters and Papers from Prison*, 177.

37. Bonhoeffer, *Letters and Papers from Prison*, 177.

38. Dilthey, *Von deutscher Dichtung und Musik.* 241–42. Bonhoeffer read Dilthey's book in prison, but only after the date of the quoted letter.

39. Bonhoeffer, *Letters and Papers from Prison*, 301.

it in front of his feet, he certainly would like to linger, to awaken the dead and to assemble what has been shattered."[40]

On 16 July 1944, Bonhoeffer once again refers to Bach in a letter to Bethge. This time in connection with one of Handel's concerti grossi to which he listened on the radio. He was "astonished once again" by how "broadly and directly" Handel "is able to offer comfort . . . in a way we would never dare to do anymore."[41] Based on this experience, which appears to make him a little embarrassed, Bonhoeffer reflects on the difference between the Handel and Bach:

> Handel is much more concerned about his listeners and the effect of his music on them than Bach. That must be why he sometimes comes across as something of a facade. Handel intends something with his music; Bach doesn't.[42]

The following question "Is that true?"[43] indicates that Bonhoeffer is not completely certain about his evaluation. However, Adorno describes what this is all about in a similar way: Bach was a "genius of remembrance." The archaic features in Bach's late work signified "the resistance to the all-pervasive commodification and subjectification" of the music, as especially visible in Handel.[44] Handel was already regarded by his contemporaries as the more modern composer because he showed more consideration for the audience's taste. But in that way the "direct comfort" that his music was able to offer according to Bonhoeffer's evaluation, was cheap comfort, comfort as a commodity. He must have had this in mind when he speaks of its "façade-like" effect.

Incidentally, Barth made a very similar distinction between Bach and Mozart, with Mozart taking the part that Bach plays according to Bonhoeffer:

40. Benjamin, "Über den Begriff der Geschichte," 697.

41. Bonhoeffer, *Letters and Papers from Prison*, 473.

42. Bonhoeffer, *Letters and Papers from Prison*, 473–74.

43. Bonhoeffer, *Letters and Papers from Prison*, 474.

44. See Adorno, "Bach gegen seine Liebhaber verteidigt" (1951), 142 and 146.

> Mozart's music is not, in contrast to that of Bach, a message . . . Mozart does not wish to say anything: he just sings and sounds. Thus, he does not force anything on the listener, does not demand that he make any decisions or take any positions . . . nor does he *will* to proclaim the praise of God. He just does it—precisely in that humility in which he himself is, so to speak, only the instrument with which he allows us to hear what he hears: what surges at him from God's creation, what rises in him, and must proceed from him.[45]

On 1 February 1944, Bonhoeffer described himself as a poor comforter: "I can listen, but I can almost never say anything."[46] It is more important for him "to really share someone's particular distress and not try to wipe it away or touch it up."[47] Instead of offering a "false kind of comfort," he prefers to "leave the distress *without interpretation* and believe this is a responsible beginning, although only a beginning, and very seldom do I get further. Sometimes I think that true consolation must come upon one unexpectedly, the same as the distressful situation did."[48] Comfort out of consideration for the suffering, comfort as commodity, would be false comfort: "cheap grace." This is what Handel's music is mostly able to give. By contrast, Bach's music, as Bonhoeffer hears it, leaves the distress uninterpreted by simply taking it in and giving it voice, by allowing us to hear what the music itself hears. In that way the possibility at least remains open that the "true comfort" can "unexpectedly break in" as costly grace; just like the chorale after the abruption of *The Art of Fugue*—maybe a poor, imperfect comfort, but certainly not a false one.

45. Barth, *Wolfgang Amadeus Mozart,* 37–38 (author's translation).

46. Bonhoeffer, *Letters and Papers from Prison,* 284.

47. Bonhoeffer, *Letters and Papers from Prison,* 284.

48. Bonhoeffer, *Letters and Papers from Prison,* 284 (italics original).

6

The Music of the Deaf Beethoven and the "New Body"

𝄞

THE CHRISTOLOGICAL CONCENTRATION OF Bonhoeffer's thinking in prison, which by then includes music, finally allows him to theologically rehabilitate the musical tradition of the nineteenth century. This goes hand in hand with his attempt in prison to rehabilitate "the bourgeoisie . . . precisely from a Christian perspective."[1] It is within this context that Bonhoeffer now also frequently mentions his Berlin teacher Adolf von Harnack, whose name had been sidelined during the "fierce" phase of the church struggle.

Writing from prison on 4 February 1944, his thirty-eighth birthday, Bonhoeffer reminds Bethge that eight years previously his Finkenwalde students had given him a recording of Beethoven's Violin Concerto in D Major as a birthday present, and that they had listened to it together. "Then I had to tell you all stories about Harnack and times past, which for some reason you particularly enjoyed."[2] Then, on 23rd February, Bonhoeffer refers to Harnack's

1. Bonhoeffer, *Letters and Papers from Prison*, 182.
2. Bonhoeffer, *Letters and Papers from Prison*, 288.

Geschichte der Akademie [History of the Prussian Academy of Sciences] in connection with his own reflections on the "fragment."[3] And, in a letter to his parents on 2nd March 1944, he refers again to Harnack's book, including reflections on tradition, especially of the nineteenth century, including music:

> I was very impressed with Harnack's history of the academy; it made me both happy and nostalgic. There are so few people today still looking for spiritual and intellectual connections to the nineteenth and eighteenth centuries; music turns to the sixteenth and seventeenth centuries for renewal, theology to the Reformation period . . . But who still has any idea of the work and accomplishments of the last century, that of our grandfathers? And how much of what they knew has already been lost to us![4]

This might have been the reason why the candidates of Finkenwalde so clearly enjoyed the stories of "times past": After all, the most recent past, which is the subject he is discussing, was fought against by the Nazis with particular intensity. For it stood not only for enlightenment and liberalism, but also for socialism and the workers' movement. Bonhoeffer then says: "I think that the day will come when people won't be able to get over their amazement at how fruitful this period was; it's so often disregarded and scarcely known."[5]

This was also true for music. Bach's *Art of Fugue,* for example, belonged to a time from which the musical youth movement no longer expected to receive any inspiration. That is why the movement preferred to go back to the time before Bach; in fact, it was a fatal misunderstanding to associate Bach's later speculative work with that period. But, at the same time, Bonhoeffer is full of enthusiasm for Mozart's "hilaritas" and also that of Hugo Wolf.[6] In addition he now also is "getting an existential appreciation of

3. Bonhoeffer, *Letters and Papers from Prison*, 305. Cf. Harnack, *Geschichte der königlich preußischen Akademie.*
4. Bonhoeffer, *Letters and Papers from Prison*, 316–17.
5. Bonhoeffer, *Letters and Papers from Prison*, 317.
6. Bonhoeffer, *Letters and Papers from Prison*, 319.

Beethoven's music from when he was deaf." We see this in his letter to Bethge of 27th March 1944 in which he refers especially to "the great set of variations from opus 111, which you and I once heard Gieseking play." As musical notation he adds the first four bars of the melody of the "Arietta":[7]

Bonhoeffer then mentions what led to his rediscovery of late Beethoven. Apart from occasionally listening to a Sunday concert on an "atrocious radio," Bonhoeffer says, "it's been a year since I heard a chorale sung." Now, as he browses through the hymn book in search of Easter anthems, he notes that "it's strange how music, when one listens with the inner ear alone and gives oneself up to it utterly, can be almost more beautiful than when heard physically. It's purer, all the dross falls away, and it seems to take on a 'new body.'"[8] In other words, Bonhoeffer observes a correspondence between the bodily resurrection, the "resurrection of the flesh" (Easter hymns!), and the music he is hearing internally. He notices that there are only "a few pieces" which he knows "well enough to hear them from within," but he could "do so especially well with Easter hymns." And it is especially within this context of Easter that he is "getting an existential appreciation" of the second (and last) movement of Beethoven's last piano sonata.[9]

In the same months of the year 1943/44 Thomas Mann, in his California exile, had conversations with Theodor W. Adorno about music, about Schönberg's twelve-tone system, and especially about Beethoven's late style.[10] These conversations are reflected in Mann's novel *Doctor Faustus*, especially in chapter 8 where Beethoven's sonata opus 111 is discussed extensively,[11] the same sonata in

7. Bonhoeffer, *Letters and Papers from Prison*, 332.

8. Bonhoeffer, *Letters and Papers from Prison*, 332.

9. Bonhoeffer, *Letters and Papers from Prison*, 332.

10. Mann, *Letters of Thomas Mann*, 2:419

11. Mann, *Doctor Faustus* 49–69.

THE POLYPHONY OF LIFE

which Bonhoeffer was particularly interested. This concurrence is so remarkable that it calls for an attempt to consider Bonhoeffer's understanding in relation to that of Adorno and Mann.[12]

In chapter 8 of *Doctor Faustus*, Mann's fictitious organist and composer, Wendell Kretzschmar, presents a lecture titled "Music and the Eye"[13] in which he says

> that music "addresses itself to the ear"; but it does so only
> in a qualified way, only in so far, namely, as the hearing,
> like the other senses is the deputy, the instrument, and
> the receiver of the mind. Perhaps . . . it was music's deep-
> est wish not to be heard at all, nor even seen, nor yet felt,
> but only—if that were possible—in some Beyond, the
> other side of sense and sentiment, to be contemplated as
> pure mind, pure spirit.[14]

Kretzschmar's "pure spirit" contemplation of music appears to be distantly related to Bonhoeffer's perception of "music heard with the inner ear," insofar as it is the "deepest desire" of music not "to be heard at all." But Bonhoeffer would hardly have spoken in the same way about a "Beyond, the other side of sense and sentiment,"[15] for what he heard was something like a "new body."

The violinist Rudolf Kolisch thought he heard in this passage from Mann's novel an echo of Adorno's understanding of "musi-cal imagination."[16] The passage in Adorno about which Kolisch is thinking corresponds almost literally with the passage quoted above from Bonhoeffer's letter: "If music, like all art, is what grand philosophy once called the sensual appearance of the idea, then musical education should first of all stimulate the ability of the mu-sical *imagination*. It should teach students to imagine music with the inner ear in such a concrete and precise way as if the sound is embodied. The faithful imagination of music is the decisive

12. See de Gruchy, "Search for Transcendence," 161–74.

13. Mann, *Doctor Faustus*, 60.

14. Mann, *Doctor Faustus*, 61.

15. Mann, *Doctor Faustus*, 61.

16. Kolisch, *Zur Theorie der Aufführung*, 11; cf. Adorno, "Zur Musikpäda-gogik" (1957) 108ff.

condition required for the tension between the spiritual and the sensual, from which music as such is living, to be carried out."[17] In contrast to Mann's novel, hearing "with the inner ear," according to Adorno, should not lead to the spiritualization (sublimation) of music but rather to a "bodily" understanding. In it a "tension" between the spiritual and sensual is carried out. This seems to correspond exactly with Bonhoeffer's experience of music receiving a "new body."

In another lecture, this time on the question, "why Beethoven did not write a third movement for the piano sonata opus 111,"[18] Mann's Kretzschmar talks about "Beethoven's art," which, in the late works, "had outgrown itself, risen out of the habitable regions of tradition, even before the startled gaze of human eyes into spheres of the entirely and utterly and nothing but personal—an ego painfully isolated in the absolute, isolated too from sense by the loss of his hearing."[19] At this point, and stronger than in Bonhoeffer, the Romantic myth of the loneliness of the genius and the triumph of the spirit over all material conditionality seems to shine through.

But Mann makes Kretzschmar clarify immediately that one should not simply equate the "idea of the merely personal" in Beethoven's later works with "limitless subjectivity" and the "radical harmonic will to expression." "As a matter of fact, Beethoven had been more 'subjective,' not to say more 'personal' in his middle period than in his last." While in the middle period Beethoven "had been far more bent on taking all the flourishes, formulas, and conventions . . . and consuming them in the personal expression, melting them into the subjective dynamic," in his late work "convention often appeared . . . untouched, untransformed by the subjective . . . in a baldness, one might say exhaustiveness, and abandonment of self, with an effect more majestic and awful than any reckless plunge into the personal." In the last piano sonatas,

---

17. Adorno, "Zur Musikpädagogik," 109.

18. Mann, *Doctor Faustus*, 51.

19. Mann, *Doctor Faustus*, 52.

for example, "the subjective and the conventional assumed a new relationship, conditioned by death."[20]

This is, of course, even to the point of being a literal formulation, an exact presentation of Adorno's 1934 essay about the "late style of Beethoven" where he says that throughout the formal language of Beethoven's work, and particularly in the last five piano sonatas, there are "conventional formulae and phrases" that Beethoven would never have tolerated during his middle period.[21] "In any case, the rule of form of his late works is of such a nature that it cannot be reduced to the concept of (subjective) expression." An analysis of these works has "to follow an idiosyncrasy, which is deliberately overlooked in the common perception, the role that conventions play in them."[22] "The relationship itself between convention and subjectivity must be understood as the rule of form, from which the content of the late works arises . . . This rule becomes manifest precisely in thinking about death."[23]

Mann then applies Adorno's understanding of Beethoven's late style specifically to the second movement of sonata opus 111. He makes Kretzschmar chant the head-motif of the "Arietta" theme, quoted by Bonhoeffer in his letter, with words of the lyrical convention, as for example: "hea-ven's blue, lov-er's pain, fare-thee well," and (as reference to the advisor Adorno's birth name "Wiesengrund"): "meadow-land."[24] Those "enormous transformations," this "mild utterance," "this pensive subdued formulation"— "Adagio molto semplice e cantabile" is the performance indication of the movement—are commented on by Kretzschmar in the course of the variation process with exclamations like "These chains of trills . . . these embellishments and cadenzas! Do you hear the conventions that are left in? Here the language is no longer— purified of the phrases but the phrases—of the appearance—of

20. Mann, *Doctor Faustus*, 53.

21. Adorno, "Spätstil Beethovens" 15.

22. Adorno, "Spätstil Beethovens," 13–14.

23. Adorno, "Spätstil Beethovens," 15.

24. Mann, *Doctor Faustus*, 54 [translation altered by Andreas Pangritz].

their subjective—domination—the appearance—of art is thrown off—at last—art always throws off the appearance of art."[25]

This is also an echo of Adorno's essay, where he writes of Beethoven's last piano sonatas that "they are full of decorative chains of trills, cadenzas and flourishes; often the convention becomes visible, bare, unconcealed, unchanged."[26] "The force of subjectivity in the late works of art is the ascending gesture, by which it withdraws from the works." Subjectivity

> disrupts them, not in order to express itself, but in order to unexpressively throw off the appearance of art . . . Therefore the conventions, which are no longer penetrated and overcome by subjectivity but left behind . . . Thus, in the late Beethoven, the conventions become expressions in the bare representation of themselves. The often-noted reduction of his style serves this purpose: it does not want to purify the musical language of the phrases, but the phrases of the appearance of their subjective domination: the liberated phrase, released from dynamics, speaks for itself.[27]

Regarding the end of the sonata Kretzschmar finally observes:

> something comes after so much rage, persistence and obstinacy, extravagance; something entirely unexpected and touching in its mildness and goodness. With this motif passed through many vicissitudes, which takes leave and so doing becomes itself entirely leave-taking . . . it experiences a small melodic expansion. After an initial C it picks up, before the D, a C-sharp . . . , and this supervening C-sharp is the most moving, consolatory, pathetically reconciling thing in the world.[28]

After this "overwhelming humanization" at the farewell, "after this detachment," a "new beginning" would be "impossible." With this conclusion the sonata had come to an end, and not only this single

25. Mann, *Doctor Faustus* 54 [translation altered by Andreas Pangritz].

26. Adorno, "Spätstil Beethovens," 15.

27. Adorno, "Spätstil Beethovens," 15–16.

28. Mann, *Doctor Faustus*, 55 [translation altered by Andreas Pangritz].

sonata but the genre of sonata "as traditional art form" had been "led to an end."[29]

In his essay on Beethoven, which Mann's Kretzschmar seems to have on his lips, Adorno has turned against the "psychological interpretation" of Beethoven's late work. In such interpretation, "in the face of the dignity of death," the theory of art "wants to resign in front of reality." Instead, Adorno suggests envisaging artificial entities [*Kunstgebilde*] themselves, in order to recognize their rule of form that becomes "manifest precisely in the thought of death."

> If, in front of the reality [of death] the right of art passes by, then [death] cannot enter immediately into the work of art as its "subject matter." [Death] is imposed upon creatures only, not to artefacts. Therefore it always appears fractured in every work of art: as an allegory.[30]

It seems that for his distinction between "creature" and "artefact" Adorno refers to a passage in Walter Benjamin's essay on Goethe's *Wahlverwandtschaften* [Elective Affinities], where Benjamin writes:

> Indeed, the artist is not so much the origin or creator, but rather he is the source or maker, and certainly his work is not his creature, but his artefact . . . It is only the life of the creature, never the life of the artefact, that has a share, an uninhibited share, in the intention of redemption.[31]

In the last resort, this kind of distinction might be a reminiscence of the biblical use of words, for in the Bible the act of "creating" (Hebrew *bara*) is reserved for God alone.

When Adorno considers the presence of death in a work of art not as a subjective premonition, but at most as an allegory, he is clearly applying Walter Benjamin's interpretation of baroque allegory as the death mask of history to Beethoven's late work. Benjamin had developed his interpretation of baroque allegory in his

---

29. Mann, *Doctor Faustus* 54 [translation altered by Andreas Pangritz].
30. Adorno, "Spätstil Beethovens," 13.
31. Benjamin, "Goethes Wahlverwandschaften," 159.

Ursprung des deutschen Trauerspiels [The Origin of German Tragic Drama], published in 1925.[32] According to Benjamin,

> in allegory the observer is confronted with the *facies hippocratica* [Hippocratic face] of history as a petrified, primordial landscape. Everything about history that, from the very beginning, has been untimely, sorrowful, unsuccessful, is expressed in a face—or rather in a death's head . . . This is the heart of the allegorical way of seeing, of the baroque, secular explanation of history as the world's history of suffering; its importance resides solely in the stations of its decline. The greater the significance, the greater the subjection to death . . . But if nature has always been subject to the power of death, it is also true that it always has been allegorical.[33]

In allegorical thinking "any person, any object, any relationship can mean absolutely anything else." This possibility implies, on the one hand, "a destructive, but just verdict . . . on the profane world," in which "the detail is of no great importance"; on the other hand, it endows "the things which are used to signify" with "a power . . . which raises them onto a higher plane, and which can, indeed, sanctify them. Considered in allegorical terms, then, the profane world is both elevated and devalued." This "dialectic of content" corresponds, on a formal level, to "the dialectic of convention and expression. For allegory is both: convention and expression; and both are inherently contradictory." In this way "the allegory is . . . not convention of expression, but expression of convention." It is "expression of authority, which is secret in accordance with the dignity of its origin, but public in accordance with the extent of its validity."[34]

Applied to Beethoven's late work, Benjamin's understanding of the allegory as death masque means that, according to Adorno, subjectivity, by withdrawing from works of art with an "ascending

---

32. Cf. Benjamin, *Origin*.

33. Benjamin, *Origin*, 166 [translation slightly altered Andreas Pangritz].

34. Benjamin, *Origin*, 175.

gesture," only leaves behind "ruins" from those works and expresses itself "only due to the cavities from which it breaks out."[35]

> But the caesuras, the sudden breaks, which more than anything else characterize late Beethoven, are those moments of outburst; the work remains silent, when it is deserted, and turns its cavity to the outside. Only then, the next fragment attaches itself, banished to its position by the commandment of the erupting subjectivity and sworn to the preceding for better or worse; for the mystery is between them, it cannot be conjured up, but only in the figure which they are forming together.[36]

The erupting subjectivity outshines the "landscape, now abandoned and alienated," with its blaze. It is through this that Beethoven's music tears the fragments "apart within time, perhaps in order to preserve them for eternity." In the history of art "late works" are thus "catastrophes."[37]

When speaking about ruins and fragments in this context, Adorno seems to refer to Benjamin's understanding of allegory as "ruin." For, according to Benjamin, "allegories are, in the realm of thoughts, what ruins are in the realm of things. This explains the baroque cult of the ruin." However, "that which lies here in ruins, the highly significant fragment, the remnant, is, in fact, the finest material in baroque creation." Benjamin observes, that

> it is common practice in the literature of the baroque to pile up fragments ceaselessly, without any strict idea of a goal, and, in the unremitting expectation of a miracle, to take the repetition of stereotypes for a process of intensification. The baroque writers must have regarded the work of art as just such a miracle.[38]

Moreover, the connection between catastrophe and preservation for eternity in Adorno's essay seems to represent another allusion

---

35. Adorno, "Spätstil Beethovens," 16.
36. Adorno, "Spätstil Beethovens," 17.
37. Adorno, "Spätstil Beethovens," 17.
38. Benjamin, *Origin*, 178.

to Benjamin's reflection on baroque allegory: "For an appreciation of the transience of things, and the concern to rescue them for eternity, is one of the strongest impulses in allegory . . . Allegory established itself most permanently where transitoriness and eternity confronted each other most closely."[39]

While reflecting on "Beethoven's music from when he was deaf," Bonhoeffer observes that "when one listens with the inner ear alone," the music "seems to take on a 'new body.'"[40] In this way he places this music like the Easter chorales of the hymnbook within the theological context of the resurrection of the flesh:

> Easter? Our thoughts are more about dying than about death. We're more concerned about how we shall face dying than about conquering death. Socrates mastered the art of dying, Christ overcame death as ἔσχατος ἐχθρός (1 Cor. 15:26). Being able to face dying doesn't yet mean we can face death. It's possible for a human being to manage dying, but overcoming death means resurrection.[41]

With the thought of resurrection, Bonhoeffer introduces a keyword, which interestingly plays an important role in Benjamin's examination of baroque allegory beside the one of death. Thus, the ruin, according to Benjamin, does not only represent transience, but at the same time the vision of something new. The ruins that antiquity bequeathed to the Middle Ages, are, for the baroque writers, "item for item, the elements from which the new whole is mixed. Or rather: is constructed. For the perfect vision of this new phenomenon was the ruin."[42] With respect to such fragmentary forms of "the preserved work of art" Benjamin even speaks of "a rebirth, in which every ephemeral beauty is completely stripped off, and the work stands as a ruin."[43] But it would be a misjudgement of the allegorical "if we make a distinction between the store of images, in which this about-turn into salvation and

39. Benjamin, *Origin*, 223–24.
40. Bonhoeffer, *Letters and Papers from Prison*, 332.
41. Bonhoeffer, *Letters and Papers from Prison*, 333.
42. Benjamin, *Origin*, 178.
43. Benjamin, *Origin*, 182.

redemption takes place, and that grim store which signifies death and damnation."[44]

It is precisely in the "visions of the frenzy of destruction," brought forth not least by the atrocities of the Thirty Years' War, "in which all earthly things collapse into a heap of ruins," that a limit to melancholic contemplation is reached:

> The bleak confusion of the field of skulls . . . is not just a symbol of the desolation of human existence. In it transitoriness is not signified or allegorically represented, so much as, in its own significance, displayed as allegory. As the allegory of resurrection. Ultimately in the deathsigns of the baroque the direction of allegorical reflection is reverted; on the second part of its wide arc it returns, to redeem. The seven years of its immersion are but a day.[45]

By the vision of the resurrection allegory finally

> loses everything that was most peculiar to it: the secret, privileged knowledge, the arbitrary rule in the realm of dead objects, the supposed infinity of a world without hope. All this vanishes with this *one* about-turn, in which the immersion of allegory . . . , left entirely to its own devices, re-discovers itself, not playfully in the earthly world of things, but seriously under the eyes of heaven.[46]

This precisely is

> the essence of melancholic immersion: that its ultimate objects, in which it believes it can most fully secure for itself that which is vile, turn into allegories, and that these allegories fill out and deny the void in which they are represented, just as, ultimately, the intention does not

44. Benjamin, *Origin*, 232.

45. Benjamin, *Origin*, 232 [translation slightly altered by Andreas Pangritz].

46. Benjamin, *Origin*, 232 [translation slightly altered by Andreas Pangritz].

faithfully rest in the contemplation of bones, but faithlessly leaps forward to the idea of resurrection.[47]

In the Easter letter from prison, where he comes to speak about Beethoven's last piano sonata opus 111, Bonhoeffer thought about the resurrection in a very similar way: "It is not through the *ars moriendi* but through Christ's resurrection that a new and cleansing wind can blow through our present world."[48] Especially in the face of omnipresent death!

It seems as if Bonhoeffer, with his "inner ear," heard in Beethoven's last piano sonata via the conversations between Thomas Mann and Theodor W. Adorno at the same time Walter Benjamin's examination of baroque mourning play [*Trauerspiel*]. In this way his Easter thoughts about "the new body" would be reconnected at the same time to his reflections on *The Art of Fugue*, whose abruption could point to a "higher perfection." And this thought would also be reconnected to his deliberations about the "O bone Jesu" by Heinrich Schütz, whose musical figures want to portray the thought of the eschatological "recapitulation." What is being suggested here, then, is a complete eschatology, formulated in musical "terms"![49]

47. Benjamin, *Origin*, 232–33 [translation slightly altered by Andreas Pangritz]. Cf. in this context Benjamin's quotation from baroque poet Lohenstein (Benjamin, *Origin*, 232): "Ja / wenn der Höchste wird vom Kirch-Hof erndten ein / So werd ich Todten-Kopff ein englisch Antlitz seyn" [Yea, when the Highest comes to reap the harvest from the graveyard, then I, a death's head, will be an angel's countenance].

48. Bonhoeffer, *Letters and Papers from Prison*, 333.

49. See Bonhoeffer, *Letters and Papers from Prison*, 336.

7

Cantus Firmus and Counterpoint

WHAT REMAINS TO BE discussed are Bonhoeffer's final theological reflections on music. These occur later than the time when Bonhoeffer first introduces his "new" theological thinking. In his letter of 30th April 1944 he had written to Eberhard Bethge: "What keeps gnawing at me is the question, what is Christianity, or who is Christ actually for us today?"[1] What followed are reflections regarding a "religionless time" and constant new questions. "How can Christ become the Lord of the religionless as well? Are there religionless Christians? If religion is only a garment of Christianity . . . —then what is religionless Christianity?"[2] This is followed by some comments on what he calls Karl Barth's "positivism of revelation": Barth had been "the only one" to have started thinking along a nonreligious line, but because of his "positivism of revelation" he had finally arrived in what is "essentially restoration." And new questions follow:

---

1. Bonhoeffer, *Letters and Papers from Prison*, 362.
2. Bonhoeffer, *Letters and Papers from Prison*, 364.

> How do we talk about God—without religion, that is,
> without the temporally conditioned presuppositions of
> metaphysics, the inner life, and so on? How do we speak
> (or perhaps we can no longer even "speak" the way we
> used to) in a "worldly" way about "God"? How do we go
> about being "religionless-worldly" Christians . . . ? In a
> religionless situation, what do ritual [*Kultus*] and prayer
> mean? Is this where the "arcane discipline" [*Arkandiszip-
> lin*], or the difference . . . between the penultimate and
> the ultimate, have new significance?[3]

Bonhoeffer returns to these Christologically motivated questions
in his letter of 5th May 1944 and in his "Thoughts on the Day of
Baptism of Dietrich Wilhelm Rüdiger Bethge" the same month.
There he sums up many thoughts formulated in connection with
his reflections on music in the previous letters. He refers to the
"vanished world" of the village parsonage and urban bourgeois
culture, the return of the past, and the fragmentation of life in his
generation. At the same time he refers to many biblical allusions
and frequently quotes the Bible, especially the Old Testament.[4]

With this context in mind, he writes to Bethge on 20th May
1944 while he is visiting Berlin and shares his thoughts about "polyphony in music." These relate to his concern to rehabilitate the
passions, especially "erotic love," and to do so Christologically. In
opposition to the exhortations of Bethge's major in Italy, who told
him "to hold out until the last man falls,"[5] Bonhoeffer defends
the right to live: "When you are in love," he says, "you want to live,
above all things, and you hate everything that represents a threat
to your life . . . However," he continues, "there is a danger, in any
passionate erotic love, that through it you may lose what I'd like to
call the polyphony of life." This allusion leads Bonhoeffer to invert
his argument:

> What I mean is that God and His eternity wants to be
> loved with our whole heart, not to the detriment of

3. Bonhoeffer, *Letters and Papers from Prison*, 364–65.
4. Bonhoeffer, *Letters and Papers from Prison*, 365–66.
5. Bonhoeffer, *Letters and Papers from Prison*, 370.

earthly love or to diminish it, but as a sort of cantus
firmus to which the other voices of life resound in counterpoint. One of these contrapuntal themes, which keep
their *full independence* but are still related to the cantus
firmus, is earthly love.[6]

During the days following, Bonhoeffer develops this "little discovery" (*Fündlein*) about the "polyphony of life" in relation to
very different human emotions. The following day, the day of his
grandnephew's baptism, in a letter to Eberhard Bethge, he writes:
"The image of polyphony is still following me around. In feeling
some sorrow today at not being able to be with you, I couldn't help
thinking that sorrow and joy, too, belong to the polyphony of the
whole of life and can exist independently side by side."[7] And again,
eight days later, he writes about Christianity, which

> puts us into many different dimensions of life at the same
> time; in a way we accommodate God and the whole
> world within us. We weep with those who weep at the
> same time as we rejoice with those who rejoice. We fear
> (I've just been interrupted again by the siren, so I'm sit-
> ting outdoors enjoying the sun) for our lives, but at the
> same time we must think thoughts that are much more
> important to us than our lives . . . Life isn't pushed back
> into a single dimension, but is kept multidimensional,
> polyphonic. What a liberation it is to be able to *think*
> and to hold on to these many dimensions of life in our
> thoughts.[8]

This multidimensionality or polyphony, which enables us to celebrate Pentecost "despite the air raids,"[9] finds its biblical justification in the other letter where Bonhoeffer writes about the "*full
independence*" of "earthly love," which is nonetheless related to the

6. Bonhoeffer, *Letters and Papers from Prison*, 393–94 [italics original;
translation slightly altered by Andreas Pangritz].

7. Bonhoeffer, *Letters and Papers from Prison*, 397. [translation altered
by Anderas Pangritz].

8. Bonhoeffer, *Letters and Papers from Prison*, 405.

9. Bonhoeffer, *Letters and Papers from Prison*, 405.

cantus firmus of the love for "God and His eternity" . . . "Even in
the Bible there is the Song of Songs, and you really can't imagine a
hotter, more sensual, and glowing love than the one spoken of here
(cf. 7:6!). It's really good that this is in the Bible, contradicting all
those who think being Christian is about tempering one's passions
(where is there any such tempering in the Old Testament?)."[10]

Bonhoeffer rejects the traditional allegorical interpretation of
this love poem from the Hebrew Bible, which in a Christomonistic
way, as always, only wants to hear *one* topic in the text: Christ and
the church, the church and Christ. But against this, he does not
offer an abstract-"secular" interpretation, which abandons Christ
and leaves the world to its own devices. He proposes, rather, a pro-
vocative Christological interpretation that makes a "true worldliness" possible, and he does so by relating all contrapuntal themes
to one cantus firmus understood in terms of Christ and towards
Christ, which gives them *"full independence"*:

> Where the cantus firmus is clear and distinct, a coun-
> terpoint can develop as mightily as it wants. The two are
> "undivided and yet distinct," as the Definition of Chalce-
> don says, like the divine and human natures in Christ.[11]

Thus, in Bonhoeffer's understanding the erotic, just as in its
autonomy, is connected contrapuntally to the love of God—in
Christ. More explicitly, he tells Bethge at the beginning of June
1944: "I'll write to you in Italy about the Song of Songs. I would
in fact read it as a song about earthly love, and that is probably
the best 'Christological' interpretation."[12] This interpretation is
a lively expression of the four negative definitions of the Chalcedonian confession of Christ, denounced as "barren"[13] in liberal

---

10. Bonhoeffer, *Letters and Papers from Prison*, 394. [translation slightly
altered by Andreas Pangritz].

11. Bonhoeffer, *Letters and Papers from Prison*, 394.

12. Bonhoeffer, *Letters and Papers from Prison*, 410.

13. This was how Adolf von Harnack, Bonhoeffer's revered teacher
in Berlin, and the leading "liberal theologian" of his time characterized the
Chalcedonian definition of the two natures of Christ. See, Harnack, *Lehrbuch
der Dogmengeschichte*, 397: "The barren, negative four definitions (ἀσυγχύτως

Protestantism. Those formulas receive unprecedented vibrancy through Bonhoeffer's musical comparison: "Is that perhaps why we are so at home with polyphony in music, why it is important to us, because it is the musical image of this Christological fact and thus also our *vita christiana*?"[14]

Certainly this is speculative thinking; however, it is not arbitrary. We may compare it with Wilhelm Dilthey's explanations about musical polyphony in his posthumously published book *Von deutscher Dichtung und Musik* (1933), which Bonhoeffer had requested in prison. According to Dilthey, "there exists between the polyphony of the Christian church music and the state of mind, whose expression it is, an inner necessary relation. The Christian-religious consciousness" lifts "the divine feeling to a mystical experience of eternity." This eternity gives "all elements of Christian consciousness its character: the need for redemption, the suffering of finitude, immersing oneself in Jesus and the spectacle of his suffering, the glad assurance of redemption." All those "conditions" exist "in their relation to the human being." They are said to be "as it were, affected, satisfied, fulfilled by the eternal experience. Polyphony gives expression to this."[15] The theology of Schleiermacher seems to shine through this understanding of polyphony as an expression of religious consciousness and the human need for redemption.

In taking sides with dialectical theology, Bonhoeffer critically distanced himself from this religious perspective. He asks: "How can Christ become Lord of the religionless as well?"[16] And this also applies to the Christian, for

---

etc.), by which allegedly everything was said, are according to the religious feelings of the classical Greek theologians deeply irreligious. They lack the warm, concrete content . . . , a theology retreating into pure negations in the issue most important for itself is doomed to failure."

14. Bonhoeffer, *Letters and Papers from Prison*, 394. [translation slightly altered by Andreas Pangritz].

15. Dilthey, *Von deutscher Dichtung und Musik*, 197–98.

16. Bonhoeffer, *Letters and Papers from Prison*, 363.

> Unlike believers in the redemption myths, Christians
> do not have an ultimate escape route out of their earthly
> tasks and difficulties into eternity. Like Christ ("My God
> . . . why have you forsaken me?"), they have to drink the
> cup of earthly life to the last drop, and only when they do
> this is the Crucified and Risen One with them, and they
> are crucified and resurrected with Christ . . . Redemption
> myths arise from the human experience of boundaries.
> But Christ takes hold of human beings in the midst of
> their lives.[17]

In contrast to Dilthey's "romantic" enthusiasm, Bonhoeffer's
Christological reflections on polyphony as a "musical image" of
a "Christological fact"[18] are clearly more sober. In this respect,
he follows the lines of Scholastic speculation about music which
goes back to the Pythagorean teachings about the "harmony of
spheres," a tradition in which all earthly music is seen as an image
of the heavenly. Thus, for example, in Rome in 1591 the musicolo-
gist Caesar Capranica, presented the following "categorization of
music":

> Music is either uncreated and divine, or created. About
> the first we confess, that it is inconceivable to human
> reason, and that it consists in the purest unity of divine
> nature and the most perfect trinity of the divine persons.
> It cannot be explained through any literal term and can-
> not be fathomed through the most thorough reflections
> of the mind. But the created music, we are talking about
> here, will be divided first of all into the observing and
> performing or into the beholding and acting.[19]

This understanding was advocated later within Protestant ortho-
doxy. In Bonhoeffer's reception, it is Christologically concentrated
and specifically applied to musical polyphony. According to his
thought, contrapuntal music like the "polyphony of life" in general, becomes "the image of the Christological fact" that in Christ

---

17. Bonhoeffer, *Letters and Papers from Prison*, 447–48.

18. Bonhoeffer, *Letters and Papers from Prison*, 394.

19. Quoted in Kirnberger, *Die Kunst des reinen Satzes in der Musik*, 176.

the divine and the human natures communicate with each other "undivided and yet different."[20]

Thomas I. Day praises Bonhoeffer's "little discovery" of the musical analogy of point and counterpoint to the Chalcedonian definition as a viable "alternative to the image of the two realms" that had been influential in Lutheran tradition and still was present in Bonhoeffer's notion of the ultimate and the penultimate.

> With his figure of the polyphonic fugue, Bonhoeffer . . . could affirm unabashed the oneness of the human life without implying its monotony. Now his notion of the ultimate and the penultimate . . . had received the corrective which would insure it meant more than a tipping of the two realms onto the time dimension. Point and counterpoint are contemporaneous, experimental in each instant.[21]

By interpreting polyphony in theological perspective, Bonhoeffer turns the Chalcedonian formulae vice versa into virtual musical movements, and this enables him to make analogical musical statements about theology that shed light on his question, "who is Jesus Christ for us today?" Already in his lectures on Christology in 1933 Bonhoeffer had seen the decisive overcoming of all "forms of thinking shaped by reification"[22] in the paradoxical, "unambiguous positive assertion about Jesus Christ" in two natures "that stand over against each other (in the Chalcedonian formula)."[23] "We are left with nothing but negations." No "positive thinking" remains possible any longer to describe what happens in the God-human Jesus Christ. This "is left as a mystery"[24] and must be understood as such. "We can only enter in faith. All forms of thought are outside the realm of possibility."[25] In a similar vein, in a newsletter from Christmas 1939, Bonhoeffer spoke about "the utmost

20. Bonhoeffer, *Letters and Papers from Prison*, 394.

21. Day, *Dietrich Bonhoeffer on Christian Community*, 195.

22. Bonhoeffer, *Berlin* 352 [translation altered by Andreas Pangritz].

23. Bonhoeffer, *Berlin*, 353.

24. Bonhoeffer, *Berlin*, 342.

25. Bonhoeffer, *Berlin*, 342.

paradox" of the doctrine of Chalcedon. "Seldom was reason so willing to humiliate itself and surrender itself before the miracle of God as happened in these words. For this very reason, seldom has reason been made into a better tool for the glorification of the divine revelation than happened then," in "reverently preserving the mystery of the person of the mediator."[26]

"The glorification" of the Christological mystery remains the driving motif of Bonhoeffer's theological thinking in prison. But now it is no longer about the surrender of reason—even though the freedom of thought is protected from arbitrariness through being bound to responsibility[27]—but about an almost-musical liquefaction, a dissolving of the dogmatic structure with the help of reason liberated to maturity: Polyphony in music as adoration, but at the same time also as an image of the "Christological fact," that in Christ God and humanity communicate with each other. In this way, the Risen Crucified One who calls Christians into the solidarity of "life on this earth," presents himself as "the human being for others" who wants to be the "Lord also of the religionless."[28]

From this perspective, some light also falls on the passages from Bonhoeffer's prison letters which Barth referred to as "enigmatic." "Now he has left us alone with the enigmatic utterances of his letters—at more than one point clearly showing that he sensed without really knowing, how the story should continue."[29] In his letters Bonhoeffer searches for an answer to his question, "who is Christ really for us today?" by working with "arcane discipline."[30] In contrapuntal music it is the cantus firmus that corresponds to the arcane (the mystery) of the person of Christ; within the

---

26. Bonhoeffer, *Theological Education Underground*, 532.

27. Cf. the "Baptismal Letter" of May 1944, where Bonhoeffer writes: "You will only think about what you have to answer for in [responsible] actions" (Bonhoeffer, *Letters and Papers from Prison*, 387). Alluding to Bonhoeffer's poem "Stations on the Way to Freedom," Bonhoeffer, *Letters and Papers from Prison*, 512–14, one could say: In thinking, too, discipline is the first station on the "road to freedom."

28. Bonhoeffer, *Letters and Papers from Prison*, 364.

29. Barth, "Letter to P. W. Herrenbrück," 90.

30. Bonhoeffer, *Letters and Papers from Prison*, 365 n. 19.

"polyphony of life" it is the thematic love of God and his eternity. But in an unredeemed world, this arcane, according to Bonhoeffer, cannot be glorified in a pure way; what counts is rather "Only he who cries out for the Jews may sing Gregorian chants."[31]

Perhaps Bonhoeffer possibly also saw in Barth's enormous dogmatic enterprise the danger of a theological "Gregorian chant," a lifting of thinking towards God irrespective of earthly suffering and human passions. We may remember in this context the opening paragraph of Barth's famous essay, "Theological Existence Today" of June 1933, where he says:

> I endeavour to carry on theology, and only theology, now as previously, as if nothing had happened. Perhaps there is a slightly increased tone, but without direct allusions: something like the chanting of the hours by the Benedictines near-by in *Maria Laach*, which goes on undoubtedly without a break or interruption, pursuing the even tenor of its way even in the Third Reich.[32]

In that case also Bonhoeffer's admiration of Barth's "hilaritas" receives a dark undertone, when he describes it "as optimism about one's own work, as boldness, willingness to defy the world and popular opinion, as the firm conviction that one is doing the world *good* with one's work, even if the world isn't pleased with it, and a high-spirited self-confidence."[33] Given the culpable failure of the church, where does Barth's theological self-assurance actually come from? Bonhoeffer's misleading accusation of Barth's "positivism of revelation" could be seen as the shadow side of what is admired as Barth's "hilaritas." In order to avoid the danger of such revelational positivism, Bonhoeffer wants to practice an "arcane discipline," a glorification of the mystery of Christ's person, whether in prayer and worship, or theological work, to which corresponds, externally, the responsible deed. In that way, the cantus

---

31. The dating of this orally handed on sentence is uncertain, but it is probably from the end of 1935. Cf. Bethge, "Dietrich Bonhoeffer and the Jews," 71.

32. Barth, *Theological Existence To-Day!*, 9.

33. Bonhoeffer, *Letters and Papers from Prison*, 319 [translation altered by Andreas Pangritz].

firmus of love for God could emerge from the arcane, within the multiple counterpoints of earthly life. These counterpoints may consist in "doing justice among human beings" and, if need be, in "waiting," until God's time comes, as Bonhoeffer wrote in his baptismal letter from prison,[34] or in suffering and, not least "earthly love," as he wrote to Bethge on 20th May 1944.[35]

Bonhoeffer's use of the analogy between Chalcedonian Christology and contrapuntal music could finally suggest a "secret affinity between the Word of God and music," in the way it characterizes the "core of Luther's theology of music" according to Oskar Söhngen.[36] Bonhoeffer was able to talk about "a certain 'affinity'" like that "between socialism and the Christian idea of the church-community."[37] But the secret "affinity" between God's Word and human music could never, if we understand Bonhoeffer correctly, be based on a "radical unity of theology and music" according to which, by nature "*all* music is related to God and therefore spiritual."[38] In contrast to such sacralization of the relative autonomy of music and worldly order in general, Bonhoeffer conceived the unity of the two "kingdoms" as being polemical, that is, as a contradictory unity. This also means music is not to be understood as derived from creation, but from Christ's lordship.

In holding such an understanding, it has to be borne in mind that the earthly-human counterpoints are not so much mere variations of the cantus firmus of love of God. The world is not to be deified; it is rather about true counterpoints, contrasts, and contradictions "which have their *full independence*." "With a really good counterpoint one should not pay attention to harmony," Arnold Schoenberg once said.[39] This sentence can be applied to Bonhoef-

---

34. Bonhoeffer, *Letters and Papers from Prison*, 390.

35. Bonhoeffer, *Letters and Papers from Prison*, 393–94.

36. Cf. Söhngen, *Theologie der Musik*, 260.

37. Bonhoeffer, *Sanctorum Communio*, 274 n. 430.

38. Söhngen, *Theologie der Musik*, 81 and 290.

39. Quote according to Adorno, "Funktion des Kontrapunkts in der neuen Musik," 157, where he comments on Schoenberg's sentence as follows: "Without any doubt Schoenberg had Bach in mind as well as his own technique."

fer's talk about cantus firmus and counterpoint: No false harmony between the divine and the human should be pretended; rather the human passions, the earthly battles for justice should go independently side by side with the theme of love for God and the glorification of the person of Christ. It is exactly in their independence that they remain counterpoints to the arcane cantus firmus. The dissonances possibly emerging from this, account for the very appeal of the music.[40] Adorno at least wanted to detect the essence of the good counterpoint in the "simultaneity of *independent* voices." "If this is forgotten, it becomes a bad counterpoint."[41]

Thus, precisely the emancipated, worldly music in its most progressive contrapuntal differentiation[42] could most likely serve as a secret reference to the mystery of the person of Christ. By completely filling the "sphere of freedom," which surrounds the area of obedience towards Christ's commandment, music acknowledges Christ's rule over the world come of age. The best witness to such "true worldliness" in music, according to Bonhoeffer, is Johann Sebastian Bach, the "genius of remembrance" (in Adorno's words)—not only as the cantor of Saint Thomas Church in Leipzig, to which conservative Lutheranism would most preferably like to pin him down, but precisely as the "worldly" composer of his late

---

40. Cf. for this already Bonhoeffer's early engagement with Karl Barth's "romantic" mixing of love of God and of neighbor in *Epistle*: "But now we are told that the essence of love for our neighbor is 'to hear in the other the voice of the One' (Barth, *Epistle*, 454, 494)." In contrast Bonhoeffer insists, "that love really does love the other, not the One in the other . . . that precisely this love for the other as other is meant 'to glorify God.'" And he continues: "Who gives Barth the right to say that the other is 'as such infinitely unimportant' (452), when God commands us to love precisely that person? God has made the 'neighbor as such' infinitely important, and there isn't any other 'neighbor as such' for us . . . But where only the one is loved in the other no communio is possible, and there the danger of romanticism ultimately creeps in" (Bonhoeffer, *Sanctorum Communio*, 169–70, note 28).

41. Adorno, *Philosophie der neuen Musik*, 56 (italics by Andreas Pangritz). "Drastic examples" are "the 'all too good' late-romantic counterpoints."

42. Cf. Adorno, *Philosophie der neuen Musik*, 60: "Polyphony is the appropriate means for the organisation of the emancipated music."

speculative works like *The Art of Fugue*.[43] After all, this work not only points through the chorale "Vor deinen Thron tret ich hiermit" [Before your throne I now appear], conveyed as the end, to the One, to whose honor alone Bach writes all his works. But rather it does so already as a contrapuntal fragment. Its political significance as resistance against the imposition of music as commodity, and as a demonstration against progressing societal conformity, appears again also in Bonhoeffer's participation in the conspiracy and resistance against the National Socialist dictatorship.

43. Adorno, "Bach gegen seine Liebhaber verteidigt," 142. Cf. also Adorno, "Bach gegen seine Liebhaber verteidigt," 138–39: "Bach is degraded by the impotent desire to just that church composer, to whose office his music defied and which he fulfilled only among conflicts . . . The reactionaries, bereft of their political heroes, take completely possession of the one, whom they have already confiscated for a long time by the name of the cantor of Saint Thomas."

Bibliography

Primary Texts

Bonhoeffer, Dietrich. *Academic and Pastoral Work: 1931–1932.* Edited by Victoria J. Barnett et al., eds. DBWE 11. Minneapolis: Fortress, 2012
————. *Barcelona, Berlin, New York: 1928–1931.* Edited by Clifford J. Green. DBWE 10. Minneapolis: Fortress, 2008
————. *Berlin: 1932–1933.* Edited by Larry J. Rasmussen. DBWE 12. Minneapolis: Fortress, 2009.
————. *Conspiracy and Imprisonment: 1940–1945.* Edited by Mark S. Brocker. DBWE 16.Minneapolis: Fortress, 2006
————. *Creation and Fall: A Theological Exposition of Genesis 1–3.* Edited by John W. de Gruchy. DBWE 3. Minneapolis: Fortress, 1997.
————. *Discipleship.* Edited by Geffrey B. Kelly and John D. Godsey. DBWE 4. Minneapolis: Fortress, 2001
————. *Ethics.* Edited by Clifford J. Green. DBWE 6. Minneapolis: Fortress, 2005
————. *Letters and Papers from Prison.* Edited by John W. de Gruchy. DBWE 8. Minneapolis: Fortress, 2010
————. *Life Together; Prayerbook of the Bible.* Edited by Geffrey B. Kelly. DBWE 5. Minneapolis: Fortress, 1996.
————. *London: 1933–1935.* Edited by Keith Clements. DBWE 13. Minneapolis: Fortress, 2007.
————. *Sanctorum Communio: A Theological Study of the Sociology of the Church.* Edited by Clifford J. Green. DBWE 1. Minneapolis: Fortress, 1998.
————. *Theological Education at Finkenwalde: 1935–1937.* Edited by H. Gaylon Barker and Mark S. Brocker. DBWE 14. Minneapolis: Fortress, 2013.

————. *Theological Education Underground: 1937–1940.* Edited by Victoria J. Barnett. DBWE 15. Minneapolis: Fortress, 2011.

Bonhoeffer, Dietrich, and Maria von Wedemeyer. *Love Letters from Cell 92: Dietrich Bonhoeffer, Maria von Wedemeyer 1943–1945.* Edited by Ruth-Alice von Bismarck. London: HarperCollins, 1994.

Supplementary

Adorno, Theodor W. "Bach gegen seine Liebhaber verteidigt" (1951). In *Kulturkritik und Gesellschaft: Prismen. Ohne Leitbild*, 138–51. Gesammelte Schriften 10/1. Frankfurt: Suhrkamp, 1977.

————. *Dissonanzen. Einleitung in die Musiksoziologie.* Gesammelte Schriften 14. Frankfurt: Suhrkamp, 1973.

————. "Die Funktion des Kontrapunkts in der neuen Musik." In *Musikalische Schriften I–III*, 145–70. Gesammelte Schriften 16. Frankfurt: Suhrkamp, 1978.

————. *Kulturkritik und Gesellschaft: Prismen. Ohne Leitbild.* Gesammelte Schriften 10/1. Frankfurt: Suhrkamp, 1977.

————. *Philosophie der Neuen Musik.* Gesammelte Schriften 12. Frankfurt: Suhrkamp, 1975.

————. *Musikalische Schriften I–III: Klangfiguren (I). Quasi una fantasia (II). Musikalische Schriften (III).* Gesammelte Schriften 16. Frankfurt: Suhrkamp, 1978.

————. *Musikalische Schriften IV: Moments musicaux. Impromptus.* Gesammelte Schriften 17. Frankfurt: Suhrkamp, 1982.

————. "Spätstil Beethovens" (1934/37). In *Musikalische Schriften, IV: Moments musicaux. Impromptus*, 13–17. Gesammelte Schriften 17. Frankfurt: Suhrkamp, 1982.

Bach, Johann Sebastian. *Die Kunst der Fuge: Ausgabe für Zwei Klaviere von Erich Schwebsch.* Berlin: Kallmeyer, 1937.

Barth, Karl. *The Epistle to the Romans.* 2nd ed. A Galaxy Book. Oxford: Oxford University Press, 1968.

————. *Wolfgang Amadeus Mozart.* Grand Rapids: Eerdmans, 1986.

————. "Letter to P. W. Herrenbrück." In *World Come of Age: A Symposium on Dietrich Bonhoefer*, edited by Ronald Gregor Smith, 89–92. London: Collins, 1967.

————. *Theological Existence To-Day! A Plea for Theological Freedom.* Translated by R. Birch Hoyle. 1933. Reprint, Eugene, OR: Wipf & Stock, 2012.

Benjamin, Walter. "Goethes Wahlverwandtschaften" (1922). In *Abhandlungen; Der Begriff der Kunstkritik in der deutschen Romantik ; Goethes Wahlverwandtschaften ; Ursprung des deutschen Trauerspiels*, 123–201. Gesammelte Schriften 1/1. Frankfurt: Suhrkamp, 1974.

————. *The Origin of German Tragic Drama.* Translated by John Osborne. London: Verso, 2009.

Bibliography

———. "Über den Begriff der Geschichte" (1940). In *Gesammelte Schriften* I/2, 691–704. Frankfurt: Suhrkamp, 1974.

Bergsten, Gunilla. "Musical Symbolism in Thomas Mann's 'Doktor Faustus.'" *Orbis Litterarum* 14/2–4 (September 1959) 206–14.

Bethge, Eberhard. *Dietrich Bonhoeffer in Selbstzeugnissen und Bilddokumenten dargestellt.* Rowohlts Monographien. Reinbek bei Hamburg: Rowohlt, 1976.

———. "Dietrich Bonhoeffer and the Jews." In *Ethical Responsibility: Bonhoeffer's Legacy to the Churches*, edited by John D. Godsey and Geffrey B. Kelly, 43–96. Toronto Studies in Theology 6. Bonhoeffer Series 1. New York: Mellen, 1982.

———. *Dietrich Bonhoeffer: A Biography.* Rev. ed. Minneapolis: Fortress, 2000.

Bloch, Ernst. *Das Prinzip Hoffnung.* 3 vols. Suhrkamp Taschenbuch Wissenschaft 3. Frankfurt: Suhrkamp, 1974.

Brodde, Otto. *Heinrich Schütz: Weg und Werk.* Kassel: Bärenreiter, 1972.

Clements, Keith. *Bonhoeffer and Britain.* London: Churches Together in Britain & Ireland, 2006.

Cobbe, Hugh, ed. *Letters of Ralph Vaughan Williams, 1895–1958.* Oxford: Oxford University Press 2008.

Day, Thomas I. *Dietrich Bonhoeffer on Christian Community and Common Sense.* Toronto Studies in Theology 6. Toronto Studies in Theology: Bonhoeffer Series 2. New York: Mellen, 1982.

Dearmer, Percy, and Ralph Vaughan Williams, eds. *The English Hymnal.* Oxford: Oxford University Press, 1906.

De Gruchy, John W. *Christianity, Art, and Transformation: Theological Aesthetics in the Struggle for Justice.* Cambridge: Cambridge University Press, 2001.

———. "The Search for Transcendence in an Age of Barbarism: Bonhoeffer, Beethoven, Mann's 'Dr Faustus' and the Spiritual Crisis of the Present Time." In *Polyphonie der Theologie: Verantwortung und Widerstand in Kirche und Politik*, edited by Matthias Grebe 161–174. Stuttgart: Kohlhammer, 2019.

Dilthey, Wilhelm. *Von deutscher Dichtung und Musik: Aus den Studien zur Geschichte des deutschen Geistes.* Leipzig: Teubner, 1933.

Duse, Ugo. "Musik und Schweigen in der Kunst der Fuge." *Musik-Konzepte, No. 17/18: Johann Sebastian Bachs spekulatives Spätwerk*, 83–113. Munich: Edition Text + Kritik, 1981.

Evangelical Lutheran Synod. *Evangelical Lutheran Hymnary.* St. Louis: Morningstar, 1996.

Grillmeier, Aloys. *Christ in Christian Tradition.* Vol. 1, *From the Apostolic Age to Chalcedon (451).* Translated by John Bowden. 2 vols. in 3. 2nd ed. Atlanta: John Knox, 1975.

Glenthøj, Jørgen. "Bonhoeffer und die Ökumene." In *Die mündige Welt: dem Andenken Dietrich Bonhoeffers*, 2:116–203. Munich: Kaiser, 1956.

Harnack, Adolf von. *Geschichte der königlich preußischen Akademie der Wissenschaften.* Berlin: Stilke, 1901.

————. *Lehrbuch der Dogmengeschichte.* Vol. 1, *Die Entstehung des kirchlichen Dogmas.* 3 vols. 5th ed. Tübingen: Mohr/Siebeck, 1931.

Hedley, William. "Vaughan Williams, the Symphony, and the Second World War." *Journal of the RVW Society* 22 (October 2001) 3–13.

Irenaeus of Lyons, Saint. *Against the Heresies.* Translated by Dominic J. Unger, OFM Cap., with further revisions by John J. Dillon. Ancient Christian Writers 55. New York: Paulist, 1992.

Kennedy, Michael. *The Works of Ralph Vaughan Williams.* Oxford: Clarendon, 1992.

Kirnberger, Johann Philipp. *Die Kunst des reinen Satzes in der Musik: aus sicheren Grundsätzen hergeleitet und mit deutlichen Beyspielen erläutert.* Berlin: Decker, 1776–79.

Kolisch, Rudolf. "Zur Theorie der Aufführung: Ein Gespräch mit Berthold Türcke." *Musik-Konzepte, No. 29/30,* 9–112. Munich: Edition Text + Kritik, 1983.

Kolneder, Walter. *Die Kunst der Fuge: Mythen des 20. Jahrhunderts.* 5 parts. Taschenbücher zur Musikuissenschaft 42–45. Wilhelmshaven: Heinrichshofen, 1977.

Leonhardt, Gustav. *The Art of Fugue: Bach's Last Harpsichord Work; an Argument.* The Hague: Nijhoff, 1952.

Maechler, Winfried. "Vom Pazifisten zum Widerstandskämpfer: Bonhoeffers Kampf für die Entrechteten." In *Die mündige Welt: dem Andenken Dietrich Bonhoeffers,* 1:89–96. 5 vols. Munich: Kaiser, 1959.

————. "Bonhoeffers Fanøer Friedenspredigt als Appell an die Christenheit heute." In *Dietrich Bonhoeffer und die Kirche in der modernen Welt* (epd-dokumentation, Nr. 2–3/1981).

Mann, Thomas. *Die Entstehung des Doktor Faustus: Roman eines Romans.* Amsterdam: Bermann-Fischer, 1949.

————. *Doctor Faustus.* Translated by Martin Secker. London: Vintage, 1999.

————. *Letters of Thomas Mann.* Vol. 2, *1942–1955.* Selected and translated from the German by Richard and Clara Winston. With an introduction by Richard Winston. 2 vols. London: Secker & Warburg, 1970.

Mellers, Wilfrid. *Vaughan Williams and the Vision of Albion.* Pimlico 23. London: Pimlico, 1989.

Moseley, David J. R. S. "'Parables' and 'Polyphony': The Resonance of Music as Witness in the Theology of Karl Barth and Dietrich Bonhoeffer." In *Resonant Witness: Conversations between Music and Theology,* edited by Jeremy S. Begbie and Steven R. Guthrie, 240–270. Calvin Institute of Christian Worship Liturgical Studies Series. Grand Rapids: Eerdmans, 2011.

Moser, Hans Joachim. *Heinrich Schütz: Sein Leben und Werk.* 2nd rev. ed. Kassel: Bärenreiter, 1954.

Müller, Hanfried. *Von der Kirche zur Welt: Ein Beitrag zu der Beziehung des Wortes Gottes auf die societas in Dietrich Bonhoeffers theologischer Entwicklung.* 2nd ed. Leipzig: Koehler & Amelang, 1961.

Bibliography

Pangritz, Andreas. *Karl Barth in the Theology of Dietrich Bonhoeffer*. Translated by Barbara and Martin Rumscheidt. 2000. Reprint, Eugene, OR: Wipf & Stock, 2018.

————. "Point and Counterpoint—Resistance and Submission: Dietrich Bonhoeffer on Theology and Music in Times of War and Social Crisis." In *Theology in Dialogue: The Impact of the Arts, Humanities, and Science on Contemporary Religious Thought; Essays in Honor of John W. de Gruchy*, edited by Lyn Holness and Ralf K. Wüstenberg, 28–42. Grand Rapids: Eerdmans, 2002.

————. *Polyphonie des Lebens: zu Dietrich Bonhoeffers "Theologie der Musik."* Dahlemer 13. Berlin: Alektor, 1994.

Pelikan, Jaroslav. *Bach among the Theologians*. 1986. Reprint, Eugene, OR: Wipf & Stock, 2003.

Scharl, Emmeran. *Recapitulatio mundi: Der Rekapitulationsbegriff des heiligen Irenäus und seine Anwendung auf die Körperwelt*. Freiburger Theologische Studien 60. Freiburg: Herder, 1941.

Schlingensiepen, Ferdinand. *Dietrich Bonhoeffer 1906–1945: Martyr, Thinker, Man of Resistance*. Translated by Isabel Best. London: T. & T. Clark, 2010.

Scholem, Gershom. "Zum Verständnis der messianischen Idee im Judentum." In *Judaica* 1:7–74. 4 vols. Frankfurt: Suhrkamp, 1963.

Schütz, Heinrich. *Erster Theil Kleiner Geistlichen Concerten*, no. 1 (SWV 282). In *Neue Ausgabe sämtlicher Werke*, 10: n.p. Kassel: Bärenreiter, 1963.

————. *Erster Theil Kleiner Geistlichen Concerten*, no. 13 (SWV 294). In *Neue Ausgabe*, 10: n.p. Kassel: Bärenreiter, 1963.

Söhngen, Oskar. *Theologie der Musik*. Kassel: Stauda, 1967.

Zimmerman, Wolf-Dieter, and Ronald Gregor Smith, eds. *I Knew Dietrich Bonhoeffer: Reminiscences by His Friends*. London: Collins, 1966.

Index

Index

Made in the USA
San Bernardino, CA
13 February 2020